FEDERAL COURTS IN THE POLITICAL PROCESS

STUDIES IN POLITICAL SCIENCE

Federal Courts
in the Political Process

By JACK W. PELTASON
University of Illinois

RANDOM HOUSE

New York

LIBRARY OF CONGRESS CATALOG CARD NUMBER 55-11752
PRINTED IN THE UNITED STATES OF AMERICA

Acknowledgments

My intellectual debt to Arthur F. Bentley and Charles B. Hagan is gratefully acknowledged. Many others have contributed to this essay, but I wish to thank especially Murray Edelman, Phillip Monypenny, Austin Ranney, Richard Snyder, and Suzanne Peltason for their comments and encouragement. Thanks are also due to the editors of *The Southwestern Social Science Quarterly* for permission to draw from a previously published article. Of course I accept full responsibility for errors and shortcomings.

Jack W. Peltason

Contents

CHAPTER ONE

The Study of Judicial Decision-Making

The purpose of this essay is to describe federal judges as participants in the political process. It is an attempt to do in a small way for federal judges what Bertram Gross and others have done more exhaustively for Congress.[1] The concern is with process rather than product. The orientation is Bentleyan, behavioristic, actional, and nonmotivational.[2]

As Tocqueville observed, "Scarcely any political question arises in the United States that is not resolved sooner or later, into a judicial question." Is it not then appropriate to describe the activity of judges in the same terms that are used to discuss legislators and administrators? In so doing we provide a common frame of description which might lead the observer to ask certain questions that might be missed in a narrower focus. Furthermore, by describing the political role of the judges, analysis of the political process will be more complete.

Studies that are primarily concerned with legal doctrines—tracing their historical development and discussing their desirability—or studies that deal with individual judges—examining the influences that molded their thoughts, discovering what they "really meant," applauding or criticizing their decisions—are very important. But these studies do not, except incidentally, provide a framework in which judicial activity can be related to the behavior of other branches of government. They still leave the judges outside the political process.

Traditional approaches to the judiciary often fail to draw attention to important data. Consider the results if the legislative process were described in the same manner as judicial activity is now detailed. Biographies of leading congressmen would be the main staple of research. Discussion of statute-making would concentrate on activity within the legislative chamber. Legislators would be seen as an isolated group. A congressman's vote, say, for the Taft-Hartley Act would be explained as reflecting his conviction that such a law was a reasonable regulation of commerce designed to promote the national interest. Studies of the legislative process would deal primarily with legislators' speeches and contain critical comments on their arguments. Attention would be focused upon formal rules of procedure. Students in courses on legislation would

be assigned readings from the *United States Code.* Little attention would
be paid to the consequences of legislative decisions.

The study of legislators as participants in the group struggle has been
fruitful. Perhaps it will be useful to study judges in the political process
also. We can find out only by trying.

Politics as Conflict of Interests

Politics can be viewed in many ways. To some it is a struggle between
the good and the bad, between the defenders of the national interest
and the spokesmen of selfish pressure groups. To others politics is the
conflict between "the people" on the one hand and "the government"
on the other. Still other students of politics assume that public officials
should be studied in terms of their motives, purposes, biases, and per-
sonalities, with only incidental reference to activity outside the formal
institutions of government.

In this essay that portion of human activity denominated "politics"
is conceptualized as a conflict among interests (or values, rights, demands). An interest consists of all kinds of activity of all kinds of people,
some of whom may be public officials, in conflict with an opposed array
of activities. For example, all the activity—talking, writing, voting,
litigating, or whatever—to secure state ownership of the oil under the
marginal seas makes up the state-control interest, which is in conflict with
the anti-state-control interest.

An interest is group activity. The activity of a single human being may
be of great significance, especially if that individual is a President,
Supreme Court justice, trade-union official, or the like. But only as the
action of that one human being is related to and supported by the
activity of others does it become relevant for our study of the political
process.

An interest gets its significance in terms of its opposite, and politics
is the process of group or interest conflict. For each interest there is
analytically established a contrary interest, although there may be little
or no activity to be observed. In such an event there is a *general* interest,
activity so widely supported that there is little or no sign of a contrary
interest within the community.

Interest is used here in a descriptive and not a normative sense. An
interest is a category used by the observer to relate and group various
kinds of activities of various kinds of people. *Special interest* refers to
the action of a part of those who make up the community. Interest does
not here mean selfish. It is not used in contrast to ideals. Hence the
term *national interest,* as used within this framework of description,
would not refer to that which the author thinks to be good for the
country, but to denote or describe activities of those who represent the
nation or those who make up the nation.

An interest is to be distinguished from a physical collection of human individuals whose aggregate activities make up the interest. More important, an interest should not be confused with a formal organization or association. For example, the Taft-Hartley-repeal interest is composed, in part, of some action of most trade-union leaders and a little action of some of their followers. It also includes the activity of many who do not belong to trade unions. On the other hand, some trade unionists' activity is part of the anti-Taft-Hartley-repeal interest. Although officials of formal associations are often active participants in interest conflicts, for some interests there is no formally organized support.

In this essay *government* denotes the activity of men known as governmental officials. These officials are described not above or outside the group conflict, but as participants in it. Their activity is interest activity. Governmental officials are to be described as representing particular interests when they act in such a way as to support that interest. The official becomes a member of the group and his action becomes a part of the interest.[3] Public officials represent many interests and are parts of many groups which may or may not be identical with or include the group which selected the officials.

Legislative votes, court decisions, presidential vetoes are to be described as interest activity. However there is no implication that these officials have "sold out to the selfish interests" or that their conduct is other than it should be. All that is noted is that when these officials make decisions, pass statutes, issue orders, write speeches, and so on, their action promotes some interests and demotes others.[4] When the United States Attorney General, for example, argued before the United States Supreme Court that public-school segregation should be declared unconstitutional, his argument was part of the desegregation interest; so, of course, was the Supreme Court decision that public-school segregation is unconstitutional and so was the opinion written to justify that decision (and so were the actions of thousands of others).

Judges in the Political Process

A judge is in the political process and his activity is interest activity not as a matter of choice but of function. Judicial participation does not grow out of the judge's personality or philosophy but out of his position. A judge who defers to the legislature is engaging in interest activity just as much as the judge who avowedly writes his own preferences into his opinions. A Supreme Court composed of Holmeses and Frankfurters would be just as much a part of the policy-making process as one composed of Sutherlands and Murphys.[5]

However, even in this enlightened day of social science one feels compelled to explain and justify an essay that attempts to describe judges and law as human institutions. Despite the washing of mechanical jurisprudence in the acid of critical observation, the notion persists that judges should not be studied in the same terms as other politicians.

James Madison long ago pointed out in *Federalist* No. 10 that the most important acts of legislation are "but so many judicial determinations . . . concerning the rights of large bodies of citizens," but students of politics, willing to describe legislators in terms of group conflict still resist applying these categories to judges. They argue that legislators are concerned with political controversies which are resolved by group struggle, but judges are concerned with legal controversies which are resolved by applying the "law."[6] Legislators choose among competing values; judges apply the law.

Of course, most political scientists and legal scholars do not believe that "the law" is an external objective phenomenon that controls judges. The traditional explanations of judicial behavior are no longer in good standing among sophisticates. Yet judges will not admit to judicial legislation and the official explanation of public men and practicing lawyers is that the law is independent of the judge and controls his behavior. This explanation is ideological, not theoretical, and although it affects conduct, it does not describe the behavior of public men, practicing lawyers, or deciding judges.

Many skeptics of the orthodox ideology, after admitting that judges sometimes do make value choices and that the law does not necessarily control judges, nevertheless explain that in most cases a properly trained judge can determine the proper rule and arrive at the correct decision by looking at statutes or at past judicial decisions. The policy-making activity of judges is thought to be an exception to the general course of judicial business and not to justify treatment of the judiciary as an integral part of the political system. Some scholars would hold that courts are political agencies when deciding constitutional questions, but should be described differently when deciding nonconstitutional matters.

It is of course true that judges make their decisions in terms of the law. The prevailing ideology requires that choices be so stated. And in many areas there is no conflict within the community about the interest to be supported. The law to be applied is clear. The judge's task is to apply rules about which there is little dispute. Judges who make decisions contrary to the widely accepted meaning of the law will discover that these decisions do not long survive. Where there is widespread agreement as to the rules which should be applied, the judge's task is relatively simple, his behavior predictable. However, whenever there is serious contention, he must choose, and he will find that he cannot turn to deductive logical machines for answers. The law becomes the judge's conclusion, not his starting point.

Compare, for example, the status of the separate-but-equal formula in 1910 with its status in the 1930s. In 1910 the formula was securely established, there was little agitation for change, the segregation interest was dominant, the law clear, the decisions predictable. By the 1930s the group struggle had unsettled the law. In 1910 there was substantial agreement on the interest to be supported, the rule or major premise was settled, and the conclusion was inevitable. By the 1930s there was conflict over the major premise, the particular interest the judge would support became less predictable. But whether the judge speaks for an interest supported by the entire community or for an interest supported by a small portion, it is necessary to describe his activities as participation in the group struggle.

More important, in order to justify an attempt to describe judges as participants in interest conflict, a discussion of whether judges discover or make law is somewhat beside the point. Whether judges make the choices or the law through the judges makes the choices, the choices are interest activity. It may be comforting to the group adversely affected to believe that the decision came not from men making value choices, but from scientific technicians. But this comfort-providing function of the official explanation of judicial behavior does not bear on or negate the importance of describing judicial choice-making in the same descriptive system used to describe other agencies of government.

To recognize that judges represent values and make choices is not to recognize that they are free to choose as they want. But then neither are legislators free. Both judges and legislators are required by the community to behave in certain ways. Both are required to explain their conduct and justify it in terms of some long-range considerations other than personal preference. A legislator explains his votes as being "required by the national interest" or "against the selfish special interests" —seldom as purely personal preferences. A judge is required to explain his decisions in terms of precedents, "intent of the framers," "intent of the legislators," "plain words of the statute." Failure to conform to the role imposed by the community can result in various kinds of sanctions.

Again, to recognize that judges participate in the political process as legislators do is not to assert that judges necessarily represent the same interests as legislators or that the consequences of judicial representation are the same as the consequences of legislative representation. Relations among judges and other decision-makers, public expectations about judicial behavior, functions allotted to judges, these and many other factors make the pattern of interest activity of judges different from that of legislators. Both judge and legislator are engaged in the group struggle, but the manner of participation varies.

Our first task will be to describe the judicial function as presently defined by the political process and to discuss the way federal judges are organized to perform their assigned tasks. Next we shall turn to the environment in which judges work. This environment includes the organizational relations among courts and other political agencies and the relations between judges and lawyers and other groups. The exact nature of these relations is established by formal organizational schemes and norms of behavior, expectations about proper conduct for judges and those who deal with them. Then we shall describe conflicts over judicial personnel, struggles to secure the support of judges, and finally the consequences which flow from the judges' activity.[7]

CHAPTER TWO

Function and Organization of Federal Judges

Among other things, federal judges appoint receivers for bankrupt businesses, preside at jury trials, admit aliens to citizenship, and so on. But their central activity is to make decisions, issue orders, and write opinions. This dispute-deciding serves a dual purpose. It helps decide controversies between the litigants and, at the same time, it is one phase in the accommodation of the interests which the litigants represent. Judges provide peaceful procedures for disposing of conflicts and they make rules that apply to many beside the immediate parties.

Judges issue orders as sanctions for their rules. Refusal to obey a judicial order or persistence in doing what the judges have labeled illegal or unconstitutional can lead to punishment.[1] Judges do not command armed forces, hence they depend on executive officials to enforce their orders, but under most circumstances there is enough support for a judicial decision that it is ignored at peril. Moreover, the impact of a court decision is not solely negative. As Professor Cahill has phrased it, "Every court decision is positive in the sense that it lends the support of the state to some interest that is seeking its protection."[2]

Because of the high prestige of federal judges and the widespread acceptance of the notion that judicial statements of right and wrong, legal and illegal, constitutional and unconstitutional, are to be given great weight, judicial opinions are important devices which both reflect and influence opinion. A trial judge's opinion is an explanation of what he decided and an argument to justify that decision. An appellate judge's opinion comprises instructions to judicial subordinates to guide them in deciding cases and is also an appeal to the reason of mankind. Judicial opinions are thought to be powerful weapons in the group struggle. Hardly a speech is made or an article written in defense of freedom of expression which does not contain a quotation from the opinions of a Supreme Court justice. Justice Holmes's comment that wire-tapping "is a dirty business"[3] was quoted no less than four times on April 8, 1954 in the House debate on wire-tapping. In summary, a judicial opinion is to interest-promotion what a movie star's endorsement is to a cigaret's sales.[4]

The functions of judges and the conditions under which they do their assigned tasks are determined by and are not above the group struggle. Governmental structure—the relations among government officials and other groups—and "the power"[5] of public officials reflect the strength of interests and are determined by the political process. Nevertheless, behavior patterns that reflect widely shared interests remain stable, so that for purposes of description they can be considered constants that channel the group contests. There is substantial agreement about the way judges should go about their tasks and about the functions they should perform. The Constitution, statutes, rules of practice, and selected portions of experience aid in defining the judicial function in contemporary United States. One of the agreed rules is the widely accepted limitation that judges decide only cases and controversies that arise in law and equity.

Scope of Judicial Power in General

Federal judges decide legal controversies. Legal controversies are those which judges decide. But rather than navigate the circumference of a tautological definition, let us examine the doctrines which purport to delineate judicial power.

DOCTRINE OF FINALITY First, there is the doctrine that finality of judgment is an essential ingredient of judicial power.[6] Thus it was decided that when a statute left the ultimate decision to the Secretary of the Treasury, judges should not determine whether persons were eligible for pensions.[7] On the other hand, judges may determine whether persons are eligible for citizenship on the advice of the Immigration and Naturalization Service since the statute provides that the final decision is to be made by judges.

The rule of finality pertains only to the formal litigants and not to the interests involved. Frequently judges have decided that some particular conduct is illegal, but the adversely affected groups have carried the battle elsewhere and have secured what amounts to a reversal of the decision. Lincoln distinguished between the finality of a decision for the litigants as contrasted with the interests when he commented: "We do not propose that when Dred Scott has been decided to be a slave by the court, we, as a mob, will decide him to be free . . . ; but we nevertheless do oppose that decision as a political rule. . . . We propose so resisting it as to have it reversed if we can, and a new judicial rule established upon this subject."[8]

Even the parties sometimes "appeal" outside the judicial forum. In *United States* v. *California,*[9] for example, after the Supreme Court decided that the national government and not the states had paramount interest in the offshore oil, the state-control interest carried the question to Congress, which reversed the impact of the Court's judgment. Thus it is only in a rather narrow focus that the rule of finality has much importance in delimiting the scope of judges' decision-making.

DOCTRINE OF POLITICAL QUESTIONS Of more significance in outlining judicial participation are the restrictions that grow out of the definition of *cases* and *controversy*. The rule is that federal judges will not decide abstract, hypothetical, or moot questions. They will not give advisory opinions, even if asked to do so by the President or the Congress, but will decide between interests only when they think it necessary to dispose of a legal case. A case, used interchangeably with controversy, is presented only when a party who has standing asserts a claim in the proper form, and presents the judges with a relatively specific issue which can be joined between two litigants who stand in an adverse relationship to each other.[10]

Judicial power is also limited by the doctrine of political questions; that is, the doctrine that courts have no authority to interfere with the discretionary authority of the other agencies of government. In most countries questions involving the constitutional competence of legislative and executive officials are adjudged to political, a notion successfully rejected by John Marshall in *Marbury* v. *Madison*. Marshall argued that in appropriate cases judges could look to the Constitution to determine if Congress or the President had authority to act.

Despite Marshall's assertion that constitutional interpretation is a legal and not a political function, over the course of years judges have refused to decide some constitutional questions and ruled that they were political. Chief Justice Taney spoke for the Supreme Court and declared that it is not part of the judicial function to determine what the Constitution means when it stipulates that the national government will guarantee to each state a republican form of government and protect the state from domestic insurrection.[11] He argued that the Constitution commits the answers to questions arising under these provisions to the discretionary authority of Congress. The Supreme Court has also decided that other constitutional questions are political, for example: those having to do with the evidence necessary to demonstrate that a statute has been enacted or a constitutional amendment ratified;[12] those arising out of foreign relations, termination of wars, or rebellions;[13] those dealing with the geography of congressional districts.[14]

From time to time, Supreme Court justices have explained the differences between a political and a legal constitutional question. These definitions of a political question often are tautological or do not square with the Court's practices. Here, for example, are three judicial definitions of political questions:

1. A political question is one which the Constitution addresses to Congress or the President rather than to courts.[15] This is a conclusion and not a formula for distinguishing between political and legal questions. Why are questions about the scope of Congress's legislative power considered legal, but questions about Congress's power to guarantee to each state a republican form of government considered political?

2. A political question involves "an appraisal of a great variety of relevant conditions, political, social and economic, which can hardly be said to be within the appropriate range of evidence receivable in a court of justice and as to which it would be an extravagant extension of judicial authority to assert judicial notice. . . ." So Chief Justice Hughes explained why questions about the "reasonableness" of the time during which states should be permitted to ratify a constitutional amendment "are essentially political and not legal."[16] On the other hand, questions which also require a consideration of a "great variety of relevant conditions, political, social, and economic" are considered to be legal—for example, the reasonableness of minimum wage laws, statutes regulating the length of trains, laws making it a crime to advocate forceful overthrow of the government to mention just a few.

3. A political question is one that "brings courts in immediate and active relations with party contests" and since "it is hostile to a democratic system to involve the judiciary in the politics of the people," judges should refrain from participating in such controversies. So wrote Justice Frankfurter in *Colegrove* v. *Green*[17] to explain why the Supreme Court would not consider whether the fifty-year failure of the Illinois legislature to reapportion the state's congressional districts violated the Constitution. However, if the Supreme Court were to refrain from deciding questions that involved the courts in the politics of the people, they would hardly be able to act. Mention any major Supreme Court decision from *Marbury* v. *Madison* through Dred Scott to the school segregation cases and one mentions a case thoroughly involved in the politics of the people. There are scores of Supreme Court decisions which have involved the Court in partisan matters.[18]

In short, political questions are those which judges choose not to decide, and a question becomes political by the judge's refusal to decide it. The refusal to decide is itself interest activity and affects the outcome of the group struggle. For example, those anxious to retain the Georgia unit system for nominating their governor won a considerable victory when the Supreme Court refused to consider the constitutionality of the scheme because it was a political question.[19] Judges, because they are judges, are involved in the politics of the people.

So far we have considered the scope of judicial power in general. However, federal judges are supposed to decide only those kinds of cases which the Constitution lists as being within the scope of the judicial power of the United States and then—with minor exceptions—only to the extent that Congress has authorized the judges to act.[20]

Scope of Federal Judicial Power

Groups which judges support support judges. Of course, the identity of groups supporting or opposing an expanded role for federal judges varies from time to time and issue to issue.[21] For example, those who favor judicial review of the decisions of the Immigration and Naturalization Service are not necessarily those who have worked to expand judicial review of the decisions of the National Labor Relations Board. But groups which expect federal judges over the long run to represent the "right" values are the groups which have favored an expansion of the role of federal judges.

By and large, the interest supporting wide participation by federal judges in the group struggle is composed of those who most fear elected and administrative officials, groups which doubt their ability to secure the selection of legislators and administrators to represent their interests. Most of the time these have been political conservatives—Federalists, slave owners, industrialists—but not always. Trade unionists, racial minorities, and civil libertarians have insisted that judges should be protected from external influence and have encouraged an expansion of their decision-making, since they argue that the judges are calm and deliberate, whereas Congress responds to pressure groups and special interests. In short, it has not been any particular economic or political faction that has championed the federal courts. Rather the interest supporting the judges is a general one.

Despite the widespread support for federal judges, there have been and continue to be conflicts over their role. Thomas Jefferson would have denied these judges the authority to declare acts of the President unconstitutional and now some southern Democrats want to take from the judges authority to decide cases involving public-school policy.[22] This is not the place for an extended description of the conflicts over the scope of federal judicial power. However, it may be useful to consider briefly one aspect of the conflict in order to illustrate how the scope of federal judicial power affects and is affected by the group struggle.

The framers of the Constitution, recognizing the strength of local sympathies and fearful that state judges might be biased in favor of the local party, made cases between citizens of different states part of the judicial power of the United States. When Congress authorized federal judges to exercise this diversity jurisdiction, it stipulated, "The laws . . . of the several states . . . shall be regarded as rules of decision in trials at common law in the courts of the United States." Then in 1842 the Supreme Court decided in *Swift* v. *Tyson* that federal judges were not in such diversity cases bound by state court decisions but should apply their own version of the general commercial common law.[23] The Supreme Court justices hoped that the state judges would follow the lead of the federal courts and there would thus be established throughout the nation a uniform set of rules covering commercial relations. However, locally elected state judges frequently represented different interests than did the federal judges, so in many states there were two versions of "the law": that applied by state judges and that applied by federal judges.

Two years after the Tyson ruling the Supreme Court reversed earlier decisions and held that a corporation was to be considered a citizen of the state in which it was chartered.[24] This permitted corporations to take advantage of diversity jurisdiction and shop around to find the judges and the law most likely to favor their cause. Federal judges gradually expanded the Tyson ruling and lawyers became artful in developing ways to create diversity of citizenship in order to permit resort to federal courts.[25]

By the 1920s diversity jurisdiction had come under increasing attack; it was alleged that it was being used to bestow special privileges on corporations. Justice Holmes wrote a series of dissenting opinions in which he argued that corporations were being allowed to escape compliance with state regulations. These opinions furnished powerful support and became an important part of the anti-Tyson and anti-diversity-of-jurisdiction interests.[26] In 1923 Mr. Charles Warren published an article in the *Harvard Law Review*[27] in which he produced evidence that Justice Story's interpretation in the Tyson case was contrary to the intention of the framers of the statute. In Congress, Senator Norris introduced and sponsored several bills designed to deprive federal courts of diversity jurisdiction. Even President Hoover came out in favor of restricting this jurisdiction.

In the face of this criticism the Supreme Court began to narrow its application of the Tyson ruling. Then in 1938, in *Erie Railroad Co.* v. *Tompkins*,[28] the Supreme Court reversed *Swift* v. *Tyson*—even going so far as to say that this decision was unconstitutional—and ordered federal judges to follow the decisions of state judges when deciding a case involving state law.

The Erie Railroad decision reduced some of the pressures against diversity jurisdiction; that is, after this decision there was considerably less activity designed to deprive federal judges of the authority to decide cases between citizens of different states. Nevertheless, the issue is not resolved and the anti-diversity interest is still substantial.

Under present legislation cases must involve in excess of $3,000 before they may be carried to federal courts on the basis of diverse citizenship. (Such cases may also be tried in state courts.) These cases provide a considerable portion of the business of federal judges. Recently the House Committee on the Judiciary recommended that the amount be raised from $3,000 to $10,000, which would preserve the advantages of diversity jurisdiction for those with large financial claims but reduce the business of federal courts.[29] Others would abolish diversity jurisdiction altogether.

Although federal judges must now decide these cases in the same manner they think that state judges would decide, corporations frequently prefer to have damage suits removed from state to federal courts in order to avoid juries from the towns in which the plaintiff resides. Furthermore in metropolitan centers federal courts are so far behind in their business that a suit can be delayed for years by this process. To quote Justice Frankfurter: "In New York, insurance companies run to cover in the federal courts and plaintiffs feel outraged by the process of attrition in enforcing their claims, due to a delay of from three to four years before a case can come to trial. . . . What is true of New York is true, in varying degrees of every big center."[30] However, in Louisiana, diversity of citizenship is now being worked to the disadvantage of insurance companies. Plaintiffs sue outstate insurance companies in federal courts and "cash in on the law governing jury trials in the federal courts, with its restrictive appellate review of jury verdicts, and escape the rooted jurisprudence of Louisiana review of jury verdicts." Justice Frankfurter commented further: "There is, to be sure, a kind of irony for corporate defendants to discover that two can play at the game of working, to use a colloquial term, the perverse potentialities of diversity jurisdiction."[31]

Organization of the Federal Judiciary

The Constitution stipulates that there shall be one Supreme Court and such inferior courts as Congress from time to time shall ordain and establish. Hence Congress (more accurately, the interests represented by a majority of Congress and the President, or two-thirds of both houses of Congress) determines not only the jurisdiction of federal courts but also their size and their kind. Although the organization of the judiciary is produced by the group struggle, for short periods the organizational scheme is a firm and fixed feature of the environment.

In both popular and scholarly literature there is a tendency to consider the justices of the Supreme Court the only judges worthy of serious attention by students of politics. The lack of concern with the work of the other judges apparently grows out of the assumption that the Supreme Court justices make policy and other judges perform the routine task of applying it.

Federal judges are organized in a hierarchical fashion with the Supreme Court at the top. But Supreme Court justices exercise much less supervision and have considerably less control over their subordinates than do most heads of corresponding pyramid-type structures. The Supreme Court majority can reverse the decisions of lower courts and criticize their opinions, but it has no formal disciplinary power over the subordinate judges, who hold office for terms of good behavior; the Constitution guarantees that their salaries shall not be reduced, and they can be neither promoted nor demoted by the Supreme Court.

Close inspection of the behavior of subordinate judges makes it evident that they represent a variety of interests, frequently interests other than those represented by the Supreme Court majority. They do not merely reflect the values supported by the Supreme Court. Furthermore, the relation is not one way; the subordinate judges are part of the Supreme Court's audience of critics. The way they formulate questions influences how the Supreme Court answers them, and they influence the flow of information up to the Supreme Court. Even if one were concerned solely with Supreme Court decision-making, it would be valuable to take into account the activities of the lower court judges.

The subordinate judge's task of applying the Supreme Court's mandates is no more mechanical than is the Supreme Court's task of applying the Constitution's mandates. The high court decisions which are supposed to guide and control the subordinates are frequently just as ambiguous as is the Constitution or statute which is supposed to guide the Supreme Court, and they admit of many interpretations. Hence, just as it is said that the Constitution is what the judges say it is, so it can be said that a Supreme Court decision is what the subordinate judges who apply it say it is.

Federal judges are grouped into two major categories, those of constitutional and those of legislative courts. The latter are created by Congress to dispose of matters that arise not within the judicial power of the United States but under some other provision of the Constitution. The Tax Court, which was established by Congress for the special purpose of hearing appeals from the rulings of the federal tax officials, is an example. In addition there is also a Court of Military Appeals which is not, according to federal statute, a "Court of the United States" at all. But this essay deals with the three major constitutional courts that are the central structure of our federal system, namely, the district courts, courts of appeals, and Supreme Court.

DISTRICT COURTS   There is at least one federal district court in each state and in some states there are four. Each district court is composed of at least one judge; in some there are as many as sixteen. Only one judge hears most cases, but sometimes three judges are necessary, for example, when someone seeks to get judges to prevent a state law from being enforced.

These judges have jurisdiction over both criminal and civil cases that grow out of federal law and, as we have noted, share with state judges authority to decide disputes involving over $3,000 between citizens of different states. In criminal cases they preside and are largely responsible for enforcing the constitutional and statutory guarantees of persons accused of crime. Trial judges spend much of their time in the application of rules on which there is substantial agreement. However, sometimes they have to choose between conflicting interests and their importance as participants in the policy process is readily attested by recalling at random the activity of Judge Goldsborough in the United Mine Workers case, Judge Pine in the steel seizure case, Judge Medina in the trial of the Communist leaders, and Judge LaBuy in the Du Pont antitrust cases.

The approximately 215 district judges consist largely of men who have been active in the political and partisan affairs of the states in which they are now serving as federal judges. Some have previously served on state courts, but an even larger number have had past legislative service. Almost all belong to the same political party and to the same faction of the political party as did the President and Senator who picked them.

COURTS OF APPEALS Athough eclipsed in public recognition by their more glamorous superiors on the Supreme Court, the approximately sixty-seven circuit judges of the eleven courts of appeals are actively engaged in making public policy. There are ten numbered courts of appeals and one for the District of Columbia, each composed of from three to nine judges, and they normally hold court in panels of three.

Although some decisions of district judges can be appealed directly to the Supreme Court, most of these decisions can be carried only to the court of appeals. In addition, these circuit judges review the actions of most of the major regulatory commissions. For example, until the orders of the National Labor Relations Board receive the imprimature of a court of appeals they may be violated with impunity. Circuit judges give more than perfunctory review to decisions of administrative tribunals. Recently some appeals courts have enforced less than 50 per cent of the Labor Board's orders which were brought to them. The Supreme Court interferes only occasionally.

A variety of interests are represented by the courts of appeals, hence there is a wide difference among the values which receive judicial support from circuit to circuit. Most of the circuit judges were active in politics prior to being appointed to the bench. A significant number are promoted from the district or state courts. Ex-law professors form a small but articulate bloc, often at odds with their colleagues who come to the bench from private law practice. Most circuit judges are Democrats, but the Republicans are gaining in number since the election of President Eisenhower. Despite the Democratic control of the national government from 1932 to 1952, there were ten Harding, Coolidge, and Hoover appointees active in 1953 when the Republican administration took over. Only one of the circuit judges, Judge Florence Allen, is a woman.

Two of the more celebrated circuit judges, Chief Judge Joseph C. Hutcheson of the Court of Appeals for the Fifth Circuit and Chief Judge Henry W. Edgerton of the Court of Appeals for the District of Columbia will serve to illustrate the diversity of interests represented by circuit judges. These men have rather wide differences as to what "the law" commands.

Judge Hutcheson was appointed to the district bench by President Wilson and elevated to the Court of Appeals by President Hoover. He started his career as a Wilsonian liberal and admired the work of Justice Oliver W. Holmes. Today he alleges, "I am, and proud of it, not a New Dealer but a Jeffersonian, Lincolnian American,"[32] and he has become critical of the philosophy of Holmes, whose followers he labeled "the sophisticated positivists, the skeptical pragmatists, the creeping socialists, and the social planners of all shades."[33]

Judge Hutcheson presides over the court of appeals which has jurisdiction over all district judges and federal administrative tribunals in Georgia, Florida, Alabama, Mississippi, Louisiana, Texas, and the Canal Zone. The judges of the Fifth Circuit tend to represent the general cluster of interests which are identified as the values of southern Democrats. The Fifth has a reputation as an antagonist of bureaucrats in general and the National Labor Relations Board (prior to its Taft-Hartley changes) in particular.[34] These judges have frequently spoken critically of some of the doctrines represented by the Supreme Court justices. For example, in 1940 when the Supreme Court censured the Fifth for refusing to give credence to the findings of fact and the rulings of the Labor Board,[35] Judge Hutcheson complained: "The inferior courts, particularly the courts of appeals, have been in the Supreme Court doghouse, the administrators in the Supreme Court parlor eating bread and honey."[36] Judge Hutcheson's opinions characterized the work of the Labor Board as "a picture of administration at its most unjudicial worst, administration which, keeping the promise of a fair hearing to the ear, breaks it to the heart." His opinions were cited by proponents of Taft-Hartley to document their criticism of the Wagner Act and to back up their charges of bias against the Board.

In 1948 Justice Douglas announced for the Supreme Court, "We have no doubt that moving pictures, like newspapers and radio, are included in the press whose freedom is guaranteed by the First Amendment."[37] Although this dictum was not made in response to the direct issue of motion picture censorship, it was a rather clear indication that the High Court was prepared at the first opportunity to reverse a 1915 decision to the contrary.[38] Yet in 1950 Judge Hutcheson, speaking for the Fifth, refused to anticipate this development and insisted upon adhering to the 1915 precedent until it was specifically overruled. He wrote, "Long-standing decisions of the Supreme Court should not be set aside by the mere personal opinion of later judges."[39] He did not mask his disapproval of the Supreme Court's use of the Fourteenth Amendment to make some of the provisions of the Bill of Rights applicable to state officers. Hutcheson argued that these decisions marked an unwarranted infringement upon the rights of local communities.

Judge Henry W. Edgerton, a former Cornell law professor who is a veteran of sixteen years on the Court of Appeals for the District of Columbia, presents a sharp contrast in interest representation to Judge Hutcheson. Edgerton, frequently in dissent,[40] has no hesitation about anticipating Supreme Court rulings on the basis of the general thrust of the high court's pronouncements. (Perhaps Judge Edgerton's approval of the general direction of the post-1937 decisions and Chief Judge Hutcheson's disapproval has something to do with their respective attitudes on this matter.) Judge Edgerton in his dissenting opinions was ahead of and pushing the Supreme Court to outlaw public-school segregation and to deprive racial restrictive covenants of judicial enforcement.[41] Judge Edgerton has also been outspoken in his belief that the Constitution requires procedural guarantees in loyalty and security hearings for federal employees.[42] He has voted, again in dissent, to apply the clear-and-present-danger test to restrict congressional investigations into questions of political belief and talk.[43]

These brief indications of the range of interests represented by circuit judges demonstrate that whether circuit judges are Edgertons, Hutchesons, or other kinds of interest spokesmen and "votesmen" makes a difference in determining who gets what, when, and where. But the interests represented by the Supreme Court justices have even greater strength.

THE SUPREME COURT The Supreme Court, composed of eight associate justices and one Chief Justice, is the most celebrated court in the world. Its prestige is unmatched by that of any other governmental agency. It is the highest judicial policy-maker in the nation and before it come parties representing most of the major interests in the country. These justices supervise the administration of justice in federal courts, arbitrate among state and national officials, and interpret the federal Constitution, laws, and treaties.

The Supreme Court has original and exclusive jurisdiction over controversies between states and all legal actions against the diplomatic representatives of foreign nations. It has original but not exclusive jurisdiction over controversies between the United States and states, actions brought by diplomatic and consular officials of foreign states, and proceedings by a state against citizens of another state or aliens. This original jurisdiction is the only authority that directly vests in any federal court. Congress may not add to or substract from this original jurisdiction, but it may authorize other courts to exercise concurrent jurisdiction.

Important as this original jurisdiction is, it is as an appellate tribunal that the Supreme Court hears most of the major interest conflicts. The Supreme Court justices review decisions of both subordinate federal courts and state courts. State judges decide cases arising under the state constitution and laws, but the Supreme Court is entitled to have the last judicial word if the interpretation and application of the federal Constitution, law, or treaty becomes involved in a case, and it is the Supreme Court which decides whether a federal question is involved.

Cases reach the Supreme Court under its appellate jurisdiction primarily either on appeal or by a petition for a writ of certiorari. Congress has stipulated that (1) if a state court declares an act of Congress or a federal treaty unconstitutional, (2) if a state court sustains a state statute against the allegation that it is in conflict with federal Constitution, law, or treaty, (3) if a district court declares an act of Congress unconstitutional in which the United States is a party, (4) if a district court enjoins the enforcement of a state statute, (5) if a court of appeals declares a state statute unconstitutional or contrary to federal law or treaty, then the disappointed litigant has a legal right to Supreme Court review which he obtains by an appeal. But in all other cases, the disappointed party merely has the legal right to file a petition asking the Supreme Court to review by issuing a writ of certiorari, a petition which the Supreme Court grants at its own discretion and in accord with its own rules.

The Supreme Court's discretion in reviewing cases on appeal is not as limited as a reading of the formal statutes and rules might indicate.[44] It is the justices who must determine if the litigant does have a right to appeal. The Supreme Court, for example, is required by statute to review decisions of state courts sustaining state statutes against the allegation that they are unconstitutional, but in recent years the justices have dismissed about half of the appeals motions on the ground that the cases involved no substantial federal question. Thus even under the appeals procedures, it is the Supreme Court which determines the cases it will consider.

Of the thousands of cases started in the United States, the Supreme Court considers closely less than 250 each year. The Court grants a petition for a writ of certiorari when at least four justices believe that the case involves special and important issues.[45] In its formal rules the Court indicates the kinds of cases which are most likely to be considered. However these rules do not tell a completely accurate story. It cannot be predicted, for example, that the Court will grant certiorari petitions even though the litigants and law review writers believe that there has been a conflict among the courts of appeals.[46] Nor does the Supreme Court consider only and all the "important" cases. Frequently the High Court leaves to subordinates the task of choosing among large interests. In recent years, for example, the Court has left unreviewed decisions of inferior judges dealing with the executive security program, investigating powers of Congress, and motion picture censorship. However, a Supreme Court decision *not* to decide is interest activity and involves the judges in the conflicts to the same extent as if the judges chose to review. Despite the judges' insistence that a denial of a petition for a writ of certiorari is not an indication of the Supreme Court's views, the effect of a denial is to support the interest represented by the decision of the court below.

Although some major questions are left to judges of inferior courts, in most instances the more controversial matters do rise to the top of the judicial structure. Two variables appear to be related to the level at which the case will be taken. First, the size of the interests represented by the formal parties: Supreme Court cases involve interests which are significantly larger in size than most of the interests represented by litigants in cases that are finally disposed of by subordinate judges. For example, when the United States government, through the Solicitor General, asks the Supreme Court to grant certiorari, it is granted in almost half the cases as compared with approximately 5 to 6 per cent of private litigants.[47] Second, the intensity of the conflict appears to be correlated with the increase in level at which a decision will be made. Cases which make the front page of a newspaper at the trial level are the ones most likely to be carried to the Supreme Court. In fact, if the case involves a large number of people and turns on an issue which these people consider important, it is predictable that not only will the case be carried to the Supreme Court, but also that the interest conflict will be adjusted in the legislative and executive arenas as well.

CHAPTER THREE

The Judicial Environment and Interest Conflict

In the previous chapter the relations among federal judges were described. But how are these judges related to other groups—governmental, nongovernmental, organized, unorganized? This pattern of relations is constantly being altered by the political process. Nevertheless, certain basic relationships have become sufficiently stabilized that they can be considered as part of the environment in which groups struggle for judicial support.

The formal constitutional provisions describe only in part the organizational relations among judges and others. It is also necessary to look at the stated norms of behavior to which judges and those who deal with them are expected to conform. But the constitutionally prescribed relations can be briefly described and it is to these that we first turn.

The framers of the Constitution, familiar with English history, had seen judges being used by kings to persecute enemies. The framers were especially anxious to establish a system in which judges would not depend upon the executive. Thus they provided that once federal judges were appointed by the President with the consent of the Senate, the judges were to serve for "good behavior" and their salaries were not to be lowered during their service.

Although judges were to be made independent, especially from the executive, the framers still left Congress and the President considerable authority to influence the general course of judicial decision-making. The President nominates judges and commands the officials on whom the judges must immediately depend for the enforcement of their orders. Congress determines the size of all courts and, except for the Supreme Court's original jurisdiction, determines what cases judges shall be permitted to decide.[1] Congress can create or abolish inferior federal courts, impeach and remove federal judges from office, and raise or fail to raise judicial salaries. Congress can by statute revise or reverse judicially developed rules, and by proposing constitutional amendments can initiate proceedings to overcome a judicial veto on constitutional matters.

The Judicial Role

However, the formal power of Congress and the President to influence the development of judicial decisions is misleading. Because of the mores of the community the judges are given an independent status which places important restrictions on Congress and the Executive. The official theory of judicial behavior is that judges stand outside the body politic. They decide cases, at least the good judges do, by a body of rules and according to the inexorable and unvarying commands of logic. They are the spokesmen for "the law." Politicians, like Congressmen and Presidents, should not interfere, for if they do, we will lose our independent judiciary and will cease to have a government of laws and not of men. Such is the core of the official theory which has wide and powerful support and requires those who would influence the judiciary to do so within the context of this belief.[2]

The judicial role imposes certain requirements upon judges. Once a man becomes a federal judge he is supposed to withdraw from active political life. Open identification with partisan controversy, contact with party or organized interest (except certain kinds which have gained "respectability") are to be avoided, and direct criticism of public officials is out of bounds.[3] Although participation in political party conflict is especially enjoined, advocating controversial causes is also looked upon with disfavor. Like an ambassador from a foreign nation, the judge is thought to be disqualified from active espousal of controversial values and it is good taste for him to confine his remarks to general sentiments. He must appear to be indifferent to the outcome of the interest struggle. As Circuit Justice Medina has remarked, "What [is] a judge to talk about when he is asked to make a speech [?] As a matter of fact, most subjects are taboo. . . . That is why you hear so many judges dive into the depths of philosophy. Whether we put you to sleep or go over your heads and flounder about, the truth of the matter is that there is seldom any alternative."[4]

Rigorous as the limitations are upon a judge's non-official conduct, they are even more stringent in connection with the judge's decision-making and opinion-writing. On the bench judges are supposed to be temperate in language and to avoid any bias as between litigants or interests. They are to phrase their decisions and explain them in a technical language which conceals any subjective element and makes the decision appear to be controlled by "the law." Similarly judges should not admit to being influenced by anything except the arguments presented in open court and the evidence presented by the attorneys and witnesses.[5] Judges are not supposed to be affected by the possible reaction to their decisions except the response of judicial superiors.[6] They are not permitted to announce how they expect to vote in advance and cannot make speeches to build support for their decisions. After a decision has been announced, judges cannot hold press conferences or write articles to explain and defend their action.[7] For this reason the *Richmond News Leader* editorialized against a proposal that the Chief Justice address Congress on the state of the Federal Judiciary as follows: "Our suspicion is that as time went on a Chief Justice . . . would stray into comment on the Court's decisions, might even feel impelled to defend certain judgments. What ever elaboration might be needed on the Court's decisions can be found—and ought to be found—solely in the written opinions of the justice."[8]

Judicial Insulation

Persons other than judges are also restrained by the mores in their dealing with judges.[9] These restraints apply not only to other governmental agencies but also to private groups. Legislators are routinely told that unless they support a particular interest they will lose some group's support. Lobbyists wine and dine legislators. But groups do not openly influence judges in this manner. The constitutional guarantee that persons have the right to petition the government for a redress of grievances is not recognized to extend to the judicial branch.

Judge Medina said: "[A citizen] should not write letters to a judge who has a matter under advisement, or in any other manner communicate with the judge to tell him how he ought to decide the case. A judge is supposed to reach his decision on the basis of what lawyers and witnesses tell him in the courtroom, not on the basis of private communications which do not form a part of the official record. This business of picketing and deluging a judge with letters and telegrams during a trial is absolutely wrong."[10] Two law professors even protested because a large number of organizations filed *amicus curiae* briefs. They gave vent to their indignation by writing: "It looked as if the situation were out of hand and the Supreme Court was being treated as if it were a political-legislative body, amendable and responsive to mass pressures from any source."[11]

So strong is the notion that it is wrong to use other than the lawyers' arguments in order to influence judges that in some jurisdictions attempts to approach judges or to influence their decision-making by tactics other than the standard legal procedures are punishable as contempt. Until a 1941 Supreme Court decision (a decision that won the support of a bare majority), state and national judges were allowed to punish persons who sought to influence a judge while a case was in process and a decision pending.[12]

CRITICIZING AND REWARDING JUDGES   The judicial role also conditions the distribution of criticism and praise. Criticism of judges, especially those on the Supreme Court, is always widespread. But the criticism takes place within the context of high public respect for the judiciary.[13] Whereas humorists, cartoonists, and public speakers are thought to be operating well within the bounds of good taste when they describe the elected officials as stumble bums without conscience and executive officers as grasping for power, convention requires that the judiciary be approached with respect and that criticism be apologetic. Those who dislike a congressional decision make no apology about saying so, but note Representative Chadwick's dilemma. He told his colleagues: "I realize that we are on delicate ground in this particular aspect of the matter. This great body has the highest respect for the Supreme Court of the United States. We all individually have that high respect, but, as attorneys we are under a special obligation of regard. Yet, as lawyers, we are inclined to feel that the Supreme Court reached an unfortunate conclusion in this [*U.S.* v. *California*] case. How we can convey that to the public and to you gentlemen without bad taste is a problem."[14]

When Professor Fred Rodell published a vigorous criticism of the Supreme Court in *Look Magazine,* Representative E. E. Cox took advantage of his congressional immunity in order to reply to what he called "cheap and villainous slander." Said the Representative: "To have named four members of this Court and charged them with incompetence, indolence, and irresponsibility is an insult to the American people."[15] Two years later another Georgia congressman made an attack on the Supreme Court which made Rodell's article look like flattery.[16] One of the congressman's fellow Representatives and supporters felt compelled to announce that despite his colleague's attack, "I know of no man who loves the courts and the judiciary more than does the gentleman who is now addressing this body."[17]

The position of judges also tempers the procedures for distributing awards as well as criticism. Judges are not allowed to receive favors openly from private groups or to receive the patronage that is available to others. About the only position to which a justice of the Supreme Court can move is the White House. Even this possibility offends some. Former Justice Roberts told a Senate subcommittee, "the Founding Fathers wanted to remove [the ambition to be President] from the minds of the Supreme Court, to make them perfectly free knowing that there was no more in life for them than the work of the Court."[18] Apparently the Founding Fathers did not make their wants generally known or clear enough, because Justice Roberts argued that the Constitution should be amended to make justices ineligible to scrve as President until five years after resigning from the bench.

An acceptable reward for judges is to make them "statesmen." Of the hundreds of men who serve on the bench, a few become statesmen. One man's statesman is not necessarily another's. In fact there is undoubtedly a fairly close correlation between the interests which a judge supports and the interests which support the judge. Justice Douglas has received awards from the Sidney Hillman Foundation, Justice Black from the Southern Welfare Conference, Justice Sutherland from Freedom Foundation Awards. Lawyers have a special role in the "statesmanizing" process and are allowed to lionize a judge more openly and with less restraint than is considered permissible for others.[19] Bar associations hold banquets and invite "honored guests." Law professors tell their students which of the judges "know the law" and which are not to be considered respectable.[20]

The insulation of judges from outside influence is one of the major distinguishing characteristics between legislative and judicial decision-makers. The very purpose of constitutional provisions, canons, and socially established rules is to minimize numbers, money, patronage, and fear of reprisal as factors influencing judicial interest representation, all factors of recognized importance in the determination of legislative behavior.

One can exaggerate the difference between the insulation of judges and legislators. Numbers do affect how judicial power will be used. Whenever an interest includes the sustained support of a considerable number of voters, it can safely be predicted that this interest will be represented by some judges. Brooks Adams, one of the more astute observers of judicial behavior, put it this way: "In fine, whenever pressure has reached a given intensity, on one pretext or another, courts have enforced or dispensed with constitutional limitations with quite as much facility as have legislatures, and for the same reasons. The only difference has been that the pressure which has operated most directly upon courts has not always been the pressure which has swayed legislatures, though sometimes both influences have combined."[21]

Yet to agree with Adams is not to agree with Mr. Dooley's celebrated dictum that "th' Supreme Coort follows th' iliction returns." On the contrary, as Professor Earl Latham indicates, evidence seems to indicate that the Court defends interests "independent of the desires of new popular majorities as reflected in the election returns or the legislation that their representatives have enacted."[22] Numbers of supporters are of less significance, designedly so, in determining how judicial power will be used than in the case of legislative decisions.[23] Judges have not hesitated to engage in conflict with the legislature, a conflict, however, which judges usually lose.

PUBLIC IGNORANCE OF JUDGES' RECORDS   The insulation of judges is related to the lack of widespread and continuous public concern about judicial activity. Except for spectacular criminal trials and a few Supreme Court decisions, news commentators and reporters who summarize the major debates in Congress and describe the daily business of government normally give less attention to judicial activity. "Inside information" about

Congress or the White House is eagerly sought, but a reporter who revealed any judicial secrets might find himself in contempt of court.

The general public lacks knowledge about the views and values represented by judges, even of those supremely significant policy-makers on the Supreme Court. Many students in college courses on American government can describe the values represented by Senator Bricker, Secretary Benson, or Congressman Taber. Yet they do not know what concepts of public interest, what values, are promoted by Justices Black or Frankfurter. Voting records of legislators are often published. Various organizations rate these records according to the degree to which they represent those organizations' concepts of the public interest. But when a scholar (Professor C. Herman Pritchett) started a vogue of publishing in popular and scholarly magazines the voting records of Supreme Court justices and arranging them according to values supported, he and his followers were criticized. Professor Mark de Wolfe Howe, for example, wrote that he doubted "whether the statistical analysis of Supreme Court opinions can, under any circumstances, be fruitful" since box scores cannot "record the impalpable factors in a process as subtle and complex as that of constitutional adjudication." The *Washington Post* commented: "We hope that Mr. Howe's exposé of this shallow thinking about the judicial process will hasten the relegation of box scores to the sports pages—where they belong."[24] Although the legislative process is as subtle and complex as that of the judicial, few have denied that something can be learned from an analysis of legislators' voting records. But to show the impact of a judge's use of his voting power, stripped of his defense of his vote, is somehow thought to be "misleading."

Lawyers in the Judicial Process

Although judges are isolated from nonjudges and although the public is generally indifferent, there is one group which makes up an important part of the environment in which judges operate. As Jeremy Bentham pointed out, "The law is not made by judge alone, but by judge and company," and of the company, the lawyers are of special significance.

Except for persons who are formal litigants, only lawyers can file briefs and directly address the judges. Great care is taken to exclude from judicial consideration all matters except those which lawyers introduce. Thus the lawyer's skill in argument, his knowledge of other decisions and ability to weave them together, and his proficiency in presenting a well-contained conclusion to the judge are factors in determining how judicial decisions are formulated. The lawyer's briefs often form the threads out of which the judge weaves his decision.

Lawyers are thought to be experts, the elite from which judges are selected, who translate and explain judicial decisions and opinions to the laymen. Lawyers consider themselves, and are frequently considered by others, to have a special responsibility for guiding the public on questions involving the Constitution and the law. The legal elite, so it is argued, serves as a vital and necessary aristocratic check on the majority. It is the lawyers' function to see that law and not men govern.

John Randolph Tucker, a distinguished attorney of his day, told the American Bar Association in 1892: "Can I be mistaken in claiming that the American Bar is and should be in a large degree that priestly tribe to whose hands are confided the support and defense of the Ark of the Covenant of our fathers, the security of which against the profane touch of open and covert foes is the noblest function and the most patriotic purpose of our great profession."[25] A more recent expression of this priestly function came from the editors of *The American Lawyer* who wrote: "It is true that vast power has been lodged in the legal profession, but that certainly does not justify the complaint that lawyers have too much power. It is no exaggeration to say that a government of laws and not of men necessarily means a government by lawyers to a very considerable extent."[26] Lawyer-spokesmen frequently quote with approval Tocqueville, who wrote that the authority Americans "entrusted to members of the legal profession, and the influence which these individuals exercise in the Government, is the most powerful existing security against the excesses of democracy."[27]

Even in the United States Senate, the lawyer-Senators consider themselves to be more expert than their nonlawyer colleagues on matters involving constitutional policy and court business and feel that nonlawyers' views on such matters are not to be given too much weight. Senator Bricker said about General Clay, cochairman of an organization to oppose the amendment sponsored by the Senator: "I have no knowledge as to whether General Clay is a lawyer. I presume he is not. I presume he is not an authority upon constitutional law. . . . We have an example in General Clay of a man who assumes to pass upon a constitutional question. I would not pass upon the manner in which General Clay conducted the Berlin airlift."[28] Opponents and proponents of the Bricker Amendment thought it important to argue that the legal profession was on their side. Senator Wiley, for example, had printed and gave great emphasis to the opinions of a large number of law-school deans who opposed adoption of the Bricker Amendment.[29] Furthermore, the nonlawyers among the Senators deferred to their legal colleagues. Senator Humphrey said, for example: "Although I am not a lawyer, yet the vast majority of lawyers who have studied the Bricker Amendment. . . ."[30]

Lawyers have a special role in selecting judges, as we shall presently note. They are also important as commentators and critics of judicial decision-making and opinion-writing. The teaching and writing lawyers have an impact upon the course of judicial decision that is hard to measure but easy to see. Writers often formulate rules, criticize past decisions, and furnish arguments for the practitioners of the bench and of the bar. The influence of Cooley, Story, and Dillon, to mention just a few, is clear.[31] Historians and political scientists join these writers in furnishing materials that sometimes find their way into the opinions.

The law reviews published by law schools, the journals published by bar associations, and professional books do for judicial decisions what the drama critics' reviews do for a Broadway play. "It was the law journals, reversing the decisions of the Supreme Court, which led the fight on the Old Court," remarks Professor Hamilton.[32] Since 1937 the law reviews have anticipated most of the changes in public policy which the Supreme Court has made. Charles Evans Hughes once said, "In confronting any serious problems, a wide-awake and careful judge will at once look to see if the subject has been discussed, or the authorities collated and analyzed, in a good law periodical."[33] As Professor Clement Vose has suggested, it may be that the Supreme Court follows not the election returns but the law reviews.[34]

The values represented by the law schools frequently differ from those supported by the bar association journals. Lawyers share a common training, speak the same technical language, owe allegiance to the same canons of conduct. Yet there are many different kinds of lawyers and it is misleading to think that they all represent the same interests. For example, there are the teaching lawyers and the practicing lawyers. Until the end of the nineteenth century, those who taught the law practiced it, but the modern law school brought specialized scholars and teachers who frequently represent interests different from those supported by such organizations as the American Bar Association.

The law reviews published by the law schools tended to be critical of the pre-1937 Supreme Court. On the other hand, the *American Bar Association Journal* tends to support the interests previously represented by the older Supreme Court. During the years 1896 to 1937, for example, the American Bar Association through its resolutions and *Journal* opposed the capital gains tax, campaigned against recall of judges, resolved that injunctions should be available in labor disputes, opposed the Child Labor Amendment, criticized the national government for relying so heavily on the income tax, and protested the growth of bureaucracy.[35] The Association opposed President Roosevelt's court-packing plan, has worked to expand the extent of judicial review of administrative agencies, has supported the Bricker Amendment, and has developed and defended the official theory of judicial power against the legal realists and modern day skeptics.

Other agencies make up an important part of the judges' company and are major adjuncts to the courts in determining the uses of judicial power. One is the Department of Justice whose decision to invoke judicial power frequently initiates significant interest conflict.[36] Other major participants are the Senate and House Committees on the Judiciary, especially the former, through whose hands pass most legislation dealing with court processes and operations. The Senate Judiciary Committee also processes all nominations to the federal bench and the late Senator McCarran, chairman of the Committee, used to refer to the judges as "my boys."[37]

By way of summary then, elaborate procedures have been established to deny groups access to the judiciary and to exclude from the judicial forum all information except that which is presented to them by the lawyers within the courtroom. The general public, although holding judges in high repute, is indifferent toward their work, and depends upon lawyers to translate the meaning and significance of judicial pronouncements. Lawyers also provide the attentive and critical audience before whom judges do their work. And lawyers are the group from which the judges come. To this we now turn.

CHAPTER FOUR

Recruiting Judges

Thousands of interest conflicts involve the federal courts. They can be conveniently discussed in terms of three general categories. First, there are the struggles to determine which men shall be the judges. Second, there are the conflicts over the judges' decision-making and opinion-writing. Finally, there are battles to implement decisions, to maximize or minimize their usefulness, and to make these decisions mean what each interest wants them to mean. The first kind of conflict is the subject of this chapter.

The decision as to *who* will make the decisions affects what decisions will be made. Although this appears obvious, during a considerable portion of our national history the fiction of judges as automatic dispensers of decisions was so strongly supported that men talked as though it made no difference who the judges were so long as they were competent legal technicians. People talked that way, but they did not act that way. There have always been struggles to secure the selection of the judge who any given group thinks is most likely to support its values.

Even today the official theory of the judiciary tends to conceal the interests conflict and makes it appear that the problem of judicial selection can best be described in terms of selection of technicians rather than policy-makers. The stress is on the necessity of "keeping the judges out of politics."

Politics and Judicial Selection

What is meant by the statement that judges should be selected without regard to politics? Some apparently mean that party politicians should have no voice in choosing judges. Others mean that Presidents, in nominating judges, should consider only the desirability of the particular candidates and exclude any consideration of paying off political obligations or building support for other programs.

The third meaning given to the demand that politics should not affect the selection of judges is that those who do the appointing should not consider whether the candidates belong to a particular political party and should not consider the values the candidate is likely to support. Rather the appointing or electing authorities should select a man with judicial temperament and sound legal knowledge. A man with a judicial temperament is defined as a man who is not committed to any particular interests and who will decide cases without respect to the consequences of his decisions.

Regardless of which meaning is intended, politics has been important in the selection of federal judges.[1] Politicians participate, obligations are paid and alliances built by passing out federal judicial positions, and great care has been taken to select men in terms of the values which they are most likely to defend on the bench. Furthermore, the accusation that the opposition is selecting judges on the basis of politics whereas one's own side selects the best men stems from the confusion as to the criteria to determine who are the best men. Beyond the obvious requirements of finding a man who is honest, has a fair degree of emotional stability, can write, and is willing to comply with the community mores, the best judge is one most likely to make the best decisions. Which are the best decisions? That is what politics is about.

John Marshall, for example, was a brilliant jurist to the Federalists but a violent and biased partisan to the Jeffersonians. Spencer Roane, Jefferson's candidate for Chief Justice, was to Jefferson an able and impartial dispenser of justice, but to the Federalists he was a prejudiced judge. In the judgment of most historians, Marshall was the better man, but the historians' judgment is based upon general approval of the interests which Marshall supported, not on Marshall's lack of partisanship or his technical knowledge of the rules of the common law. Similarly, prior to 1937 those who objected to the conservative majority on the Supreme Court accused these judges of being intemperate partisans who wrote their own views into the law. Since 1937 those who dislike the values supported by the justices have charged the judges with being politicians.

Despite the political nature of the selection process, despite the fact that judges, especially those of our higher federal courts, have as much to say about the group struggles as do legislators,[2] the entire selection process is surrounded by conventions which make it difficult to discuss openly the conflict of values. A candidate for Congress seeks group support, makes pledges and discusses how he will vote if elected. Various organizations endorse or oppose legislative candidates without apology. But when it comes to selecting judges, the candidates are not supposed to discuss publicly how they will decide cases or indicate the interests they will represent if chosen for the bench. It is even considered inappropriate for Senators who must approve the nominations to question the candidates too closely about their position on constitutional or legal questions.[3] Rather, the hearings are in terms of bar association endorsements and testimonials by various individuals dealing with the integrity and honesty of the candidates. Recently concern about the candidates' "Americanism" has actually meant some inspection of the candidates' values. Nevertheless the discussions still turn primarily on "judicial temperament" and "legal ability." Yet the actual contests turn on anticipations as to the interests which the candidate is most likely to represent.

Appointing Judges

The Constitution calls for the President to select federal judges with the consent of the Senate. But the Constitution does not give an accurate description of the selecting process, especially of district judges. It would be more accurate to say that federal district judges are selected by the individual Senator or local party organization in the area which they are to serve, subject to presidential veto. Judgeships are important senatorial patronage and the Senate seldom fails to confirm any man acceptable to the individual Senator from the state in which the judge is to serve. It always fails to confirm if the man is unacceptable to the individual Senator, provided the Senator belongs to the same political party as the President. If the judge is to serve in a state in which there is no Senator who belongs to the same party as the President, the President has greater freedom in picking the judge, but he usually does so in consultation with local party officials.

FACTORS CONSIDERED   Party considerations are most important. Since 1885 over 90 per cent of all federal judges have been filled by members—in most cases active members—of the same party as the President who chose them and most have been supporters of the Senators who nominated them. When Grover Cleveland became President the federal bench was solidly Republican. No Democrat had been appointed to the Supreme Court since 1861. Cleveland appointed thirty-seven judges, all Democrats except one independent, and a Mugwump who had supported Cleveland. When Harrison became President the federal bench was 65 per cent Republican, but Harrison overcame this imbalance (from his point of view) of so many Democrats; of twenty-nine judges he nominated, twenty-six were Republicans. McKinley choose twenty-two Republicans and one Democrat. Theodore Roosevelt appointed seventy-two new federal judges of whom sixty-nine were Republicans, two Democrats and one independent. When Taft became President, a man who more than any other President supported the "official theory" and who was opposed to mixing politics and the judiciary, 90 per cent of the federal bench was Republican. Taft named forty-five new judges of whom thirty-seven were Republicans and eight were Democrats. But five of these eight Democrats were in the South where the whole bar was Democratic and, as Taft said, it was impossible to name Republicans. Wilson made seventy-two original appointments, seventy-one Democrats and one Republican, and was able to turn over to Harding a federal bench composed about 50 per cent of Democrats and 50 per cent Republicans. Under Harding the federal structure was "modernized and reformed" and twenty-five new judgeships were created to which twenty-five Republicans were appointed. During his relatively short time in office Harding named forty-three Republicans and one Democrat to the federal bench. Coolidge appointed sixty-one Republicans and seven Democrats and Hoover chose forty-two Republicans and seven Democrats so as to turn over to President Roosevelt a federal court system composed 90 per cent of Republicans. By 1944 Roosevelt had selected 106 Democrats and two independents. President Truman followed the same pattern to turn back to President Eisenhower a federal judicial structure composed chiefly of Democrats. Since 1952 President Eisenhower has been helped by the establishment of fifteen additional judgeships, and the creation of a number of vacancies by Republican judges who have felt it safe to resign when, finally, there was a Republican in the White House. As of February 1954 President Eisenhower had chosen only two Democrats and these were southerners who had supported the President in the 1952 election.[4]

As the low men in the judicial hierarchy district judges are not as important in the final disposition of interest conflict as are their superiors. On the other hand, there are a large number of district judgeships which function in particular states so that they are useful to reward faithful service, gain support from various factions, even to get rid of possible political antagonists. Thus in the selection of district judges Presidents have paid somewhat more attention to party and less attention to values likely to be supported than has been the case in the selection of circuit and Supreme Court judges. In addition individual Senators have more voice in selecting district judges than they do in choosing those higher up the ladder.

Promotion from district to circuit judge is not uncommon, but promotion from circuit judge to the Supreme Court is unusual. Furthermore, the importance of Supreme Court justices in determining which interests shall get their way has made it less likely that these positions will be filled in order to build support. Rather, care has been taken to select men who will promote the same concepts of the public interest as are held by the President. Some Presidents have been more successful in predicting how the men they select will act as judges than have others. Theodore Roosevelt took unusual pains to be sure that he was getting men who could be "counted upon," even going so far as to seek assurances that his nominees would vote right if chosen.

The Senate does not take lightly its responsibility to confirm nominees. The procedure normally followed in selecting district and circuit judges is for the Attorney General, the Senator from the state in which the judge is to function, provided he belongs to the President's party, and the

American Bar Association's Committee on the Federal Judiciary to consult with one another. The President then nominates a candidate who is given a full Federal Bureau of Investigation check, the file being made available only to the Chairman of the Senate Committee on the Judiciary. Routinely the Senators from the state in which the judge is to sit are notified and wires are sent to the representatives of the state and local bar associations asking for their views on the nominee.[5] In the event that any objections are heard a public hearing is likely to be held.

Lawyers play a leading role in the selection of federal judges. The Canons of Legal Ethics stipulate that since "lawyers are better able than laymen to appraise accurately the qualifications of candidates for judicial office,"[6] the lawyers have a positive duty to speak out. Since knowledge of the law is thought to be important in determining the judge's decisions, only lawyers are chosen, although there is no constitutional requirement to this effect.[7] Furthermore, the spokesmen for the bar are deferred to by laymen in the selection of candidates. The Senate Judiciary Committee is composed solely of lawyers. Senators are hesitant to recommend men whom the leaders of the bar would condemn as unfit and such action by the bar associations reduces the nominees' chances of getting confirmed. Recently the Attorney General has gone so far as to submit the names of all candidates, except for the Supreme Court, to the appropriate committee of the American Bar Association before sending the nomination to the Senate. The Senate Judiciary Committee always asks for the Bar Association's opinion.

Despite the important position of the bar, the present system does not give the leaders of the American Bar Association as much authority as some would like. Mr. Loyd Wright, a member of the American Bar Association Committee, for example, is quite disturbed by the fact that the Committee's recommendations are sometimes not followed[8] and he charged that to have politicians select the judges destroys the independence of the courts. He told the Senate Judiciary Committee, "This great arm of government is being prostituted by the politicians who have the right of the appointing power."[9] Professor Joseph P. Harris is another who believes that the bar should be given more of a voice. He has written that under the present system "it is not uncommon for nominations to be given to politician-lawyers of little standing at the bar, who have secured the necessary political support."[10] Apparently instead of the support of politicians, Professor Harris would prefer to require the support of the leaders of the bar. However, it is doubtful if the Senators and the interests they represent would be willing to give up their present patronage. If they did, it would transfer to the bar association the struggles to select the "right" men and would alter the nature of the interests represented by judges, probably in the direction of the interests supported by the *American Bar Association Journal*.

TWO CASE STUDIES[11]   In 1916 the Supreme Court was participating without apology or restraint in the major clashes among interests. Groups whose interests were defeated in the legislature carried the battle before federal judges and discovered that the judges could be counted upon to label some of the unwanted legislation unconstitutional or at least interpret it in such a way as to leave the maximum area of conduct unregulated. The balance among the justices was close. Then in 1916 President Wilson nominated Louis D. Brandeis to fill the vacancy created by the death of Justice Lamar.

By 1916 Brandeis was a well-known campaigner for vigorous governmental regulation of utilities, for savings-bank insurance, against bigness, and for conservation. He had been active before the Supreme Court and had successfully persuaded the judges to sustain laws limiting hours of work. Quite clearly Brandeis's nomination presented a threat to those interests that had been most successful in securing judicial representation from the 1890s.

Opposition to Brandeis was phrased not in terms of his views but of his supposed lack of judicial temperament. On the other hand Brandeis's supporters also played down his values since they did not want to lose the support of the southern Democrats on the Judiciary Committee. Each side sought testimonials from distinguished members of the bar. Each side accused the other of representing a selfish special interest.

The Senate Judiciary Committee held public hearings. Leading the opponents were some distinguished attorneys, including five former presidents of the American Bar Association. President Lowell of Harvard, heading a list of fifty-five Bostonians—where Brandeis lived—wrote: "We do not believe that Mr. Brandeis has the judicial temperament and capacity which should be required in a judge of the Supreme Court. His reputation as a lawyer is such that he does not have the confidence of the people."[12] Bishop Cannon, leader of the prohibition groups, also testified against Brandeis. On the other side, supporting him, were representatives of trade unions, some distinguished Bostonians, Harvard President-Emeritus Eliot for example, and, most important, the President of the United States.

Brandeis himself, although careful to comply with the conventions that require the nominee not to seek confirmation openly, was "accidentally" brought into contact with two doubtful Senators and was able to win their support. The election of 1916 was approaching and President Wilson was able to rally the members of his own party. Finally, on the vote to confirm, although all the Republicans opposed, all the Democrats plus three Progressives voted for Brandeis.

The opponents of John J. Parker who was nominated to the Supreme Court in the spring of 1930 were more successful. At the time of his nomination Judge Parker had served for five years on the Court of

Appeals for the Fourth Circuit. Prior to this, he had been active in North Carolina Republican politics. Parker's nomination was opposed by the leaders of the American Federation of Labor and the National Association for the Advancement of Colored People. Spokesmen for the NAACP emphasized that when campaigning for governor in 1920, Parker had responded to the charges that the Republican Party intended to enfranchise the Negro by saying, "The participation of the Negro in politics is a source of evil and danger to both races and is not desired by the wise men in either race or by the Republican Party of North Carolina."

The American Federation of Labor based its opposition on an opinion Parker had written for the circuit court in the Red Jacket case.[13] A lower court had issued an injunction against a union for trying to persuade workers who had signed yellow-dog contracts to join the union. Parker voted to sustain the lower court on the ground that the Supreme Court's decision in the Hitchman case[14] required him to do so. The leaders of the American Federation of Labor thought otherwise. Other members of the anti-Parker interest included Progressive Republicans, Republican Senators from states with large Negro and labor votes, and a majority of the Democratic Senators. There were enough of these to block the nomination.

The bitter debates over Brandeis and Parker were unusual. Presidents normally are careful to choose men who have not aroused any major group and therefore likely to be confirmed readily. The most "available" man is one who has had noncontroversial public service.

Creating Vacancies

The personnel of federal courts is altered not only when a judge is selected to fill a vacancy, but also by the devices used to create vacancies. Vacancies are made whenever a judge dies, resigns, retires, is impeached and removed, or when Congress creates or abolishes judicial positions. All but one of these procedures gets rid of an incumbent as well as making an opening available.

Assassination of judges has not been used in the United States as a weapon in the interest struggle. But judicial ability to stay alive has had an important impact on the kinds of interests represented by federal courts. Judicial longevity has been remarkable. Nevertheless, since 1900 every President has been able to appoint at least one member of the Supreme Court and all except McKinley, Coolidge, and Eisenhower (up to the spring of 1955) were able to appoint at least three justices.

IMPEACHMENT The Constitution gives federal judges tenures of "good behavior," but stipulates that they can be impeached by a majority of the House of Representatives and removed from office by two-thirds of the Senate for "treason, high crimes and misdemeanors." The first attempt to remove a federal judge by this procedure came in 1803 when the Republican majority successfully impeached and removed Judge John Pickering for insanity. Two years later the Republicans, angered by the behavior of Federalist judges, impeached Supreme Court Justice Samuel Chase. Chase had actively participated in the campaign for Adams, had vigorously applied the Sedition Laws to Republicans, and in his charges to grand juries had criticized Congress and Jefferson for their equalitarian slogans and legislative programs.

Some Republicans argued that judges should be removed whenever they represented interests contrary to those of the congressional majority. Congress, they said, represents the majority of the electorate and unless objectionable judges could be removed, the judges would dominate the majority. Other Republicans, although not willing to go this far, believed that open partisanship from the bench, even though short of illegality, justified Chase's removal.

The Federalists rushed to Chase's defense. They argued that the only ground on which a judge could be removed was for offenses that were criminal at common law. John Marshall, who believed he would be the next target, went so far as to suggest that it would be preferable to give Congress authority to reverse a Supreme Court decision rather than to remove the offending judges. (This was just two years after Marshall had asserted the doctrine of judicial review in *Marbury* v. *Madison.*) But despite some strong White House pressures, the Republicans failed by four votes to remove Chase. (The Federalists also turned back an attempt of the Republican-controlled Pennsylvania legislature to remove Federalist state supreme court judges.)

Only four federal judges have been removed by impeachment and eight have resigned to avoid trial.[15] Congress has been willing to vote for removal on the basis of unethical conduct even if it is not illegal. Although impeachment has not been of major importance, because of the growth in prestige of the federal judiciary and the development of the ideology that it is improper for Congress to influence judicial decision-makers, threats of impeachment are not infrequent.

Representative Rankin told his colleagues that every judge who votes against segregation should be impeached.[16] After Judge Kaufman presided over a trial which failed to bring in a conviction of Alger Hiss, he was subjected to severe criticism and accused of bias and improper conduct by Congressmen Nixon, Case, Walters, Cox, Macy, Dondero, Keffe, and others, some of whom urged his impeachment.[17] When the Court of Appeals ruled by a two-to-one vote that Harry Bridges was entitled to bail, Senator Langer, then ranking minority member of the Senate Judiciary Committee, submitted a resolution calling for a thorough investigation. He said, "If the facts in the Bridges case are as they have been stated to me, Judges William Orr and William Healy should be impeached and thrown out of office."[18] And, said the Senator, other judges "who might be sympathetic to Russian Communism" should also be thrown out of office. When Justice Douglas stayed the execution of Soviet espionage agents, he aroused the ire of a considerable number of Congressmen, one of whom introduced a resolution for impeachment.[19] Other such threats could be mentioned. Nevertheless, despite the intense criticism and severe opposition that judges have faced, the interest against impeachment of federal judges has been dominant throughout most of our history.

It seems plausible that the failure to develop impeachment as a device to remove unpopular judges contributed to the demand for electing state judges for short terms. In the early decades of the twentieth century agricultural and labor organizations championed the recall of judges and judicial decisions and gained success in a few states. In the 1912 campaign Theodore Roosevelt endorsed recall of judicial decisions, to the great anguish of President Taft, but the proposals to make federal judges elective for short terms have never had much support. However, efforts to restrict judicial tenure by getting judges to resign or retire have been plentiful.

RESIGNATION AND RETIREMENT Jefferson found the judiciary manned by Federalists, Lincoln discovered it to be dominated by Democrats, Cleveland found the judges were all Republicans. Judges, appointed years before, often have different conceptions of the Constitution than do the President or the congressional majority. They interpret the statutes to support values other than those represented by Congress or the President. These judges are obstructions to the President. But the judges sometimes view the passing of the older order as a calamity. Throughout our history judges have attempted to keep the judiciary in safe hands by timing their retirements in order to deny their opponents a chance to appoint their successors.

The anguish of Marshall and Story over the gradual change in the federal judiciary is matched by the fears of other judges who have witnessed their political enemies capture control of the elective branches and threaten the judiciary. Chief Justice Taney stayed on the bench long after he was frail and thus prevented Lincoln from nominating a Republican successor. Ben Wade said, "No man ever prayed as I did that Taney might outlive James Buchanan's term . . . but now I am afraid I have overdone it."[20] Justice Nathan Clifford stayed on the Court and clung to life hoping for the Democrats to return to power. Professor Fairman has written that Clifford felt a "sacred trust to use what power he had to keep alive the flickering flame of the faith to which his first and abiding allegiance had been sworn."[21] In 1929 Chief Justice Taft wrote, "I am older and slower and less acute and more confused. However, as long as things continue as they are, and I am able to answer in my place, I must stay on the court in order to prevent the Bolsheviki from getting control. . . ."[22] By 1937 President Roosevelt was the only President except Johnson who had served a full term without having a single vacancy to fill on the Supreme Court, despite the fact that there were several rather elderly men on the bench.

Legislation designed to make it easier for judges to resign or retire normally comes after a political party returns to power. In 1869 a statute was passed which permitted federal judges who reached the age of seventy and who had ten years of service to resign at full pay. The inducement to get judges to leave the bench created opportunities for President Grant to insure that the interests of the Radical Republicans would be adequately supported. In 1913, a year after the Democrats returned to power, Attorney General McReynolds proposed that when any judge, except justices of the Supreme Court, failed to take advantage of the retirement provisions, the President should be authorized to appoint an additional judge to sit in that court. Democratic Attorneys General renewed this proposal for the next five years. In 1916 the Senate approved but the House rejected by a narrow vote. Then in 1919 a statute was passed that allows the President to appoint additional inferior court judges for those eligible to retire, but only if the President finds the incumbent judge is unable to discharge effectively the duties of his office because of mental or physical disadvantage.

In 1937 when President Roosevelt found that the federal courts represented anti-New Deal interests and consisted of judges who were refusing to resign, he proposed that if judges who were eligible chose not to resign or retire the President be allowed to appoint additional men.[23] Congress refused to agree. The most recent encouragement to retire came in February 1954 when the Republican-dominated Congress reduced the retirement age to sixty-five for judges with fifteen years' service.

From time to time there have been suggestions that the Constitution be amended to compel judges to retire at a certain age. In April 1937 when the bench was predominantly Republican and a Democrat was in the White House, an American Institute of Public Opinion poll showed that 65 per cent of the Republicans opposed such an amendment, but 80 per cent of the Democrats approved. But in 1954 it was the Republicans in the Congress who pushed a provision to compel federal judges to retire at age seventy-five, provided they had served for at least ten years. In 1954 the federal bench was overwhelmingly Democratic and a Republican was in the White House.

CREATION AND ABOLITION OF JUDGESHIPS   One of the easiest ways to secure representation is to create some new judgeships and then appoint the "right men." When the Federalists lost the election of 1800, but before they had to turn the government over to the Jeffersonians, they created sixteen new judgeships. They also reduced the size of the

Supreme Court from six to five members to deprive the incoming President of a chance to make an appointment in the event of a vacancy.

Jefferson, who was not, as we have seen, overawed by judicial authority, recommended to Congress that the Judiciary Act of 1801 be reconsidered. The Republicans argued that since Congress could create inferior federal courts, it could also abolish them, and proceeded to do so. The Federalists protested that this violated the constitutional guarantee of life tenure for federal judges because the judges of the abolished courts were out of jobs. But the Federalists protested in vain. To make it less likely that the Federalist judges would declare the 1802 Repealing Act unconstitutional, the bold Republicans passed a law to provide for annual instead of semiannual sessions of the Supreme Court, which postponed the Court's meeting for an entire year. The Federalist judges acquiesced in this assertion of congressional authority, but Marshall struck back the next year with *Marbury* v. *Madison*.

Congress did not abolish a federal court again until 1911. In June 1910 Congress created at President Taft's suggestion a Commerce Court of five judges to have exclusive jurisdiction to review the decisions of the Interstate Commerce Commission, a Commission whose authority had been curtailed by judges and then reasserted by Congress.[24] The "insurgent" liberal Republicans and Northern Democrats opposed the establishment of a special court because of the fear that the judges would favor the railroads and curtail the authority of the Commission. Despite this opposition the court came into being. The judges as predicted began to reverse the Commission's rulings and to curb its activity. Other judges had done this before the creation of the special Commerce Court. But the creation of a special court just to review the Commission's decisions spotlighted judicial opposition. Although the Supreme Court frequently reversed the Commerce Court, this merely added to the criticism and the movement to abolish the court began to gain strength.

By December 1911 Democrats had control of the House and were able to attach a rider to an appropriation bill to abolish the court. In the Senate there was an extended debate over what should happen to the five judges if the court were abolished. Senator Sutherland of Utah quoted from Story to argue that not only would it be unconstitutional to abolish the position of the judges but also to abolish the court. Despite the opposition of the Taft Republicans, the Senate concurred with the House, but with the provision that the judges would be retained as ambulatory circuit judges.

President Taft felt so strongly about the attempt to abolish the Commerce Court that he used his veto, even at the expense of the appropriation measure, and in a strongly worded message to Congress spoke out against the growing volume of criticism of federal judges, criticism supported by Theodore Roosevelt who had put forward the idea of popular recall of judges. President Taft returned the measure to the House with the statement, "I am utterly opposed to the abolition of a court because its decisions may not always meet the approval of a majority of the Legislature."

The opponents of the Commerce Court were unable to override the President's veto. But their criticism became even more intense when the Supreme Court ruled that the Court could not review the Commerce Commission's dismissal of a complaint.[25] The consequence of this decision was to deny shippers a review but to give the railroads an opportunity to seek review when the Commission held against them.

Just about this time Judge Archibald of the Commerce Court was impeached, an action enthusiastically supported by the Court's critics. Then came victory for the Democrats in the 1912 elections. The opponents of the court pushed through a statute calling for its abolition. (The House wanted to abolish the judgeships also, but finally decided otherwise.) Wilson signed and, after less than three years, the Commerce Court was abolished.

When a court of general jurisdiction acts, the complex of interests which judges perforce represent tends to obscure the judges' function as interest representatives. Under such conditions it is apparently more difficult for interests adversely affected to mobilize against the offending judges than is true if the judges (or administrators) have specialized jurisdiction. The establishment of a court with specialized jurisdiction to decide a single major interest conflict brings to public attention the judicial participation in interest disputes and the particular interests the judges support are difficult to hide. Specialized administrative tribunals frequently get the reputation of being more biased than courts for the same reason that the Commerce Court got into difficulty.

CHANGING THE SIZE OF COURTS   Less dramatic than the creation or abolition of courts, but of more significance, has been the routine creation of new judgeships and the expansion in the size of existing courts. Changes in the size of the Supreme Court have caused considerable controversy. At the district and circuit level, the expanding population and growth of judicial business have led to a constant increase in the number of judges, but most increases have come after a party has long been out of power. During Harding's first administration, for example, after the Republicans had been out of office for eight years, they made up for lost time by creating twenty-five additional judicial positions. This was followed by more additions so that by the end of the Coolidge Administration the size of the federal judiciary had been about doubled. Again in 1954 Congress authorized thirty additional judicial positions and appropriated money for fifteen of these to which "deserving Republicans" were appointed.

The Federalists' reduction in the size of the Supreme Court in 1801 from six to five, and then the Republicans' increase back to six has already been noted. In 1807 the size was increased to seven, which gave Jefferson a chance to make two appointments. In 1837 the Court was enlarged to nine and Jackson appointed two strong states' rights men, a move which further reduced the influence of Marshall's constitutional supporters. In 1863 the Supreme Court was increased to ten, partly to allow Lincoln to be assured that his war policy would not be judicially attacked. As Lincoln told Congressman Boutwell when he appointed Chase to be Chief Justice, "We wish for a Chief Justice who will sustain what has been done in regard to emancipation and legal tender." (Lincoln guessed wrong on Chase and legal tender.)

After the Civil War the Radical Republicans in control of Congress fought to prevent President Johnson from making appointments to the Supreme Court. They rejected his nominees and reduced the size of the Court from ten to eight. Thus despite three vacancies due to deaths and resignations, Johnson made no appointments.

When Grant replaced Johnson, Congress increased the size of the Supreme Court to nine, provided for nine new circuit judges, and, as we have noted, encouraged existing judges to resign by providing full pay for those who reached seventy and had ten years of service. Because of the increase in the size of the Court and resignation of the aged Justice Grier, Grant chose two justices. The Senate rejected one of his nominees and the other died four days after confirmation. In the meantime the Supreme Court declared the Legal Tender Act of 1862 unconstitutional by a vote of four to three.[26] A few hours after this decision was handed down, Grant nominated two men[27] who a year later joined with the three Republican dissenters to reverse the earlier legal tender decision.[28]

In 1937 President Roosevelt attempted to increase the size of the Supreme Court to a maximum of fifteen by adding one justice for every one who was over seventy and had ten years of service but who refused to retire. This attempt is too recent to need much comment. The design of the President's proposal was clear. But so strong was the conviction that it is wrong to influence judicial decision-making that the President chose to wrap his proposals in the language of efficiency. He argued that federal judges were falling behind in their business. Despite the President's popularity and despite the general agreement among his supporters that the Supreme Court should not be allowed to block the New Deal, interests supported by the Court majority were able to defeat the President's proposals. The justices themselves played a leading role in fighting the President. Chief Justice Hughes and Justice Brandeis wrote a letter defending the Court against the charge that it was inefficient, one of the conservative justices announced his retirement at a crucial time, and between March and June of 1937 the Supreme Court altered the interests it supported. When the justices began to support New Deal measures, it became less necessary to pack the Court.[29]

The various attempts to alter the size of the Supreme Court in order to alter the interests supported by the justices have alarmed those who believe that this loophole undermines the independence of the courts. The American Bar Association and Senator Butler of Maryland have recently sponsored a constitutional amendment to fix the size of the Supreme Court at nine. Although approved by the Senate in 1954, the Amendment did not get to the floor of the House.[30]

To summarize, conflicts over personnel of federal courts have involved battles to influence presidential appointments and senatorial confirmations; impeachment; resignations and retirements; abolishing, creating, and altering the size of courts. In these struggles groups are required to conform to the stated norms and formulate their arguments in terms of accepted conventions such as "selecting the best man," or "improving the efficiency of the court system," or "preserving the independence of the courts." The desire to influence personnel of the courts in order to get judicial support for particular interests of a more specific nature is seldom stated openly. Yet to the observer of the political process, conflicts over the recruiting of federal judges must be taken into account if explanations are to approach completeness.

CHAPTER FIVE

Securing a Decision

The personnel of the federal courts is relatively stable and groups must seek representation of their interests by judges as they are rather than with judges as they might be. Groups that fail to dominate the selection of judges are at a disadvantage, but they are not necessarily destined to have their interests unrepresented. Judges are not completed products at the time of their selection, who thereafter merely "play out" the interests within them. Like all human beings, they alter and are altered by events.

If attention is too narrowly focused, connections between actions outside and inside the courtroom may be overlooked. For example, the Supreme Court decision in *Southeastern Underwriters*,[1] bringing the insurance business within the scope of the antitrust acts, was not an isolated event. Rather it was preceded by demands of congressmen for the regulation of insurance, by state officials agitating for national action, by Temporary National Economic Committee investigations. After failing to win congressional support necessary to amend the statutes, the group supporting regulation did get the Department of Justice to prosecute under existing statutes. In Congress the antiregulation group countered with speeches about states' rights and bills to exempt the insurance industry from the antitrust laws.[2] The Supreme Court decision was but a small part of a whole cluster of intense activity. It must, as any Supreme Court decision, be explained not as an isolated event but as part of a stream of interest conflict.

In this chapter the broad outlines of the relations among groups and judges will be sketched in order to describe how groups invoke judicial power and seek representation. Groups seeking judicial support do so within the context of a structured situation where the alternatives are limited. They may not seek direct access. They must speak through the lawyers, the professional judicial persuaders. Appeals must be couched in the technical language and formulated in terms of precedents, intent of the framers, and demands of justice. If groups are to be successful, they must act in accord with the official ideology discussed in Chapter Three.

This chapter is not designed as a manual on how to influence judges, nor is it concerned with the judges' internal thought processes. Rather it is a discussion of participation in the group struggle. Groups do certain things; judges make decisions and write opinions. It is the non-judges who usually take the initiative.

Entering the Judicial Forum

When and how do groups enter the judicial forum? Not always deliberately. It is necessary to see the distinction between the formal parties to a legal controversy and the interests they represent. A litigant represents and is part of an interest, but should never be confused with the whole interest. A decision has consequences for others—sometimes thousands of others—not immediately before the court. Thus the action of the litigants is but one small segment of all the activity which makes up the interest represented.[3] For example, when Allwright, a Democratic election judge, refused to allow Smith to vote in the Texas Democratic primary because Smith was a Negro, Smith sued Allwright, alleging that Allwright's conduct deprived Smith of rights guaranteed by the Constitution and federal laws. The judges formulated the immediate question in terms of whether Allwright was liable for damages. But the judges were choosing not only between Smith and Allwright, but between the values these men represented; and the judges' decision created a rule of law which affected millions of people.[4]

Judicial power is frequently invoked by parties for reasons that have nothing to do with the promotion of large values. For example, a man on trial for murder may raise the claim that he was denied his constitutional right to the assistance of counsel and in so doing represent an interest of a much wider scope than he himself is aware. His own reasons for his activity may be unrelated to, and certainly not designed to promote, any wider interest.

But whether judicial power is invoked deliberately to promote a large interest or to defend a personal cause, it is necessary that the parties proceed according to certain established steps and in accord with certain requirements. The details of judicial procedure need not detain us here. Our concern is with the judiciary as a policy-making arena and not with detailed knowledge of courtroom procedures.[5]

INVOKING JUDICIAL POWER Judges may not normally initiate judicial proceedings. Rather the parties who have a grievance must take the first step. Just as only congressmen have "standing to introduce," so interests must find a person who has what is technically known as "standing to sue" if they desire judicial activity. In the case of nongovernmental persons, one must persuade the judges that he is about to or already has sustained a real and substantial injury for which the law provides a remedy. A general concern as a citizen or taxpayer is not enough. Justice

Frankfurter phrased it as follows: "We can only adjudicate an issue as to which there is a claimant before us who has a special, individualized stake in it. One who is merely the self-constituted spokesman of a constitutional point of view cannot ask us to pass on it."[6]

Government prosecutors are of especial importance in initiating judicial action. They guide the grand jury, assert rights in behalf of the national government, and enforce the thousands of federal statutes. Because there are so many statutes, the prosecutors have wide discretion in determining which ones they shall enforce. In areas like antitrust and civil rights where there remain major interest conflicts over the kinds of behavior which are enjoined, the prosecutor's decision to prosecute marks an important stage in the policy-making process. The Civil Rights Section of the Department of Justice, for example, has been an important representative of the civil rights interests. Unable to secure representation by a majority of Congress, but supported by the Executive, the civil rights interest initiated prosecutions under the existing federal statutes and have had considerable success in expanding the area of federal protection.[7]

Groups other than the formal parties are sometimes permitted to file briefs before appellate courts and to argue in behalf of their causes. In the years immediately prior to 1949 when the Supreme Court freely permitted the filing of *amicus curiae* briefs, there were a large number filed each term. When some Hollywood writers contested the power of Congress to punish recalcitrant witnesses, forty organizations filed briefs.[8] Then in 1949 the Supreme Court amended its rules. Governmental units may still file briefs as a matter of right, but other groups can do so only with the consent of both parties or by a motion showing that the brief to be submitted will cover materials not adequately presented.[9] Despite the ruling, the number of *amicus curiae* briefs continues to be significant.

Whoever invokes judicial power must follow certain procedures. As we have noted, federal judges require an adversary proceeding in which two litigants genuinely contest each other's claims. Furthermore, the issue must be presented to the judges in such a way that a decision is thought to be necessary in order to dispose of the controversy between the parties of record.

These limitations have not provided a serious restriction upon the entering of the judicial forum. Judges have not been hesitant about participating in interest disputes. For each rule there are exceptions. Despite the rule that there must be parties with an adverse interest, and in the face of a statute forbidding injunctions against the collection of any tax, the anti-income tax interest was able to get a case before the federal courts challenging the 1894 income tax. Two stockholders brought action against their own respective corporations, alleging that the corporation should be enjoined for dissipating the company's assets and prevented from paying an unconstitutional tax. The Supreme Court majority agreed.[10] Likewise a president of a coal company was allowed to sue his own company and the other officials (including his father who was a vice-president of the company), in order to prevent them from complying with the Guffey Coal Act which the company president alleged was unconstitutional.[11] In 1953 the Supreme Court permitted a white man to raise the argument that damages assessed against him would violate the rights of Negroes, this despite the rule that one cannot assert the rights of another.[12] Dred Scott furnishes another case in which the adversity of interests can be questioned and it is doubtful if Marbury really wanted his commission.[13] In short, as Tocqueville observed a hundred years ago, "Scarcely any political question arises in the United States that is not resolved sooner or later, into a judicial decision."

SELECTING THE RIGHT CASE   In addition to maneuvering to get the issue before the judges, it is desirable to get the right case at the right time. The defenders of the National Industrial Recovery Act were outmaneuvered when they allowed those attacking the statute to bring the issue before the Supreme Court in a case involving the actions of some chicken commission men in Brooklyn.[14] The entire NRA program was debated in terms of the impact of the actions of these small merchants on interstate commerce. The anti-NRA interest had a more persuasive case than they might otherwise have had if the railroad or coal producers were before the judges. On the other hand, the first case in which the Wagner Act was challenged involved a major steel producer. The Chief Justice speaking for the Court majority said, "When industries organize themselves on a national scale, making their relation to interstate commerce the dominant factor in their activities, how can it be maintained that their industrial labor relations constitute a forbidden field into which Congress may not enter when it is necessary to protect interstate commerce from paralyzing consequences of industrial war?"[15] Then this decision was cited to support the Wagner Act's application to a clothing manufacturer and other companies that could hardly be described as organized on a national scale.[16]

The conflict between power companies and the TVA furnishes another interesting illustration of tactics.[17] After the companies were defeated by legislation they turned to litigation. A group of preferred stockholders of the Alabama Power Company introduced the litigation by asking a federal district judge to enjoin the company and TVA from performing under a contract that called for the company to sell transmission lines to TVA and which divided Alabama territory between the company and TVA.

The power companies attacked the whole plan of TVA and argued that the entire scheme was unconstitutional. Spokesmen for the TVA insisted that the single question for the judge was whether the government could sell power produced at Wilson Dam, a dam originally authorized as a military project and completed long before TVA was established. But the district judge granted a sweeping injunction against the TVA. However, on review the Supreme Court narrowed the question to the legality of the contract and sustained the power sale and purchase of transmission lines.[18]

Nineteen power companies then joined forces and prepared to do battle again. The power companies' strategy was to try the issue in a Tennessee state court and to avoid federal judges who already had ruled adversely to them. On the other hand, the tactics of TVA counsel were to get the question before federal judges, whom they thought would be more likely to favor the TVA. The companies moved first and filed identical suits, one in federal court for northern Alabama and the other in a Tennessee state court. The federal case was to be saved in the event that the Tennessee case was dismissed for lack of venue or jurisdiction. But TVA attorneys acted to forestall this maneuver by filing a complete answer to the charge in the state courts—which would take a long time—and merely a motion to dismiss the complaint in the federal court—which would bring the issue to trial before federal judges in a hurry. The power companies then decided to risk dismissing the Alabama suit and thus left the issue to be decided solely by state judges. But TVA took advantage of diversity jurisdiction and had the case removed to the federal district court in Tennessee. This marked a partial victory for the power companies who, although unable to avoid federal judges, had been able to avoid those in Alabama.

Finally the federal district judge in Tennessee granted a sweeping preliminary injunction against TVA activity. But the circuit court of appeals reversed, sent the case back, and told the judge to hear the evidence before acting. Meanwhile the Judiciary Act of 1937 became law, requiring a three-judge court whenever an injunction is sought against enforcement of a federal law. The district judge who granted the first injunction was joined by two other judges who, after a long trial, ruled in favor of the TVA. On appeal to the Supreme Court, the justices decided that the power companies had no standing to contest the issue and that the constitutionality of TVA had not been properly before the courts[19] (who by this time had decided that the TVA was constitutional).

Litigation over the Public Utilities Holding Company Act provides a final example of how various interests seek the right case in which to secure judicial support. After the passage of the Act, utilities sought injunctions all over the country. The government attorneys were very anxious to limit the first case which would test the constitutionality of the Act to the registration requirements, and then the other provisions of the Act could be tested separately. They also wanted a test case that involved a large holding company system, in order to demonstrate effectively the practices which had led to the enactment of the statute. To accomplish these objectives all government officials—postal, prosecutors, Securities and Exchange Commission—were told to refrain from any step to enforce the Act while the government pressed forward a case designed to compel Electric Bond and Share Company to register.

The utilities, on the other hand, were searching for a case which from their point of view was best designed to attack the statute. They wanted a sweeping ruling against the whole system. Finally they got a bond-holder of a bankrupt company to request the judge to require the company to be liquidated since, it was argued, the Holding Company Act required this to be done. To secure an adverse interest, another creditor contested the bondholder's claim. He agreed that the Holding Company Act required liquidation but alleged that the statute was unconstitutional.

Counsel for the Securities and Exchange Commission rushed to urge the judge to dismiss the constitutional argument. They argued that the two creditors did not have an adverse interest, had not adequately disclosed the facts, and had misconstrued the Act. They introduced evidence that one of the creditors had signed a document to permit his name to be used but that he did not know who was representing him, had made no arrangements for payment of counsel, had no interest adverse to that of the other party.

The district judge ruled that the entire statute was unconstitutional. The circuit court of appeals sustained the decision. Both parties, that is, the two creditors, joined to ask the Supreme Court to grant certiorari. The government filed a memorandum urging the Supreme Court to deny the petition, claiming once again that it was a trumped-up case and that judicial power had been improperly invoked. The Supreme Court agreed with the government and refused to consider the case.

Meanwhile the Electric Bond and Share Company case was being decided. The company wanted the whole Act to be declared unconstitutional, but the Commission was successful in keeping the issue confined to the registration provision and was able to bring the narrow issue before the Supreme Court as the first test case of the Act.[20] In summary, the Supreme Court majority participated as part of the pro-Holding Company Act interest, but the district and circuit judges had represented the anti-Holding Company Act interest.

To Seek or Not to Seek a Decision

THE ANTISEGREGATION INTEREST   In this section the activity that has made up the antisegregation and laissez-faire cluster of interest will be used to illustrate tactics and strategy of groups seeking judicial support. It is inaccurate to identify antisegregation as the Negro interest because the conflict is not between Negroes and whites. Most, but not all, Negroes, it is true, participate in the antisegregation interest. The activity of whites is less uniform, some supporting the desegregation and some the segregation interest.

After the Civil War the desegregation interest included for a time a majority of the Congress, which made it a federal crime for state officials or private individuals to discriminate against Negroes. But the segregationists, an interest that has long included an overwhelming majority of the public officials of Southern states, scored major victories when the national Supreme Court either ruled that these laws were unconstitutional or narrowly construed them.[21] By 1876 the segregationists were powerful enough to prevent any congressional action. The executive branch ceased to support actively the desegregation interest and federal civil rights statutes fell into disuse.

In 1896 the segregationists scored a major legal victory when the Supreme Court decided that states could require by law that Negroes be segregated in places of public accommodation, schools, recreational and transportation facilities provided equal public-supported facilities were made available to Negroes.[22] Only one Supreme Court justice participated as a desegregationist.[23] This interest had lost representation in Congress, the presidency and the Supreme Court. From 1868 to 1936 fourteen Supreme Court decisions involved attempts to secure to Negroes the right to use the same facilities as whites, but in only two of these were the claims upheld. Furthermore, the Supreme Court refused to review many other decisions of subordinate judges who supported segregation.

By the 1930s, the desegregation interest had grown and its leadership had become more aggressive. What were the alternative kinds of action open to the desegregationists?

1. A constitutional amendment to make it unconstitutional for either public officials or those who operate public facilities to make any racial classifications? The advantages of such an amendment were clear, but the segregation interest was too large and had too much support in Congress and state legislatures to make success by this procedure probable.

2. Congressional action, perhaps a statute denying federal funds to states that segregated, or more effective federal civil rights statutes? Again, the segregationists had enough strength, especially in the Senate, to block any such legislation.

3. State legislative action? State legislatures had constitutionally recognized authority to pass statutes outlawing segregation and in some states they established antidiscrimination commissions. But in the areas where segregation was the most strongly entrenched, the segregationists dominated the legislature.

4. Action by the state judiciaries? These judges could interpret their own constitutions or the federal Constitution and could construe statutes so as to restrict segregation. But state judges represented approximately the same interests as did the state legislatures—with some notable exceptions, in California, for example.

5. Action by the President? As commander-in-chief he could abolish segregation in the armed forces; as chief administrator he could restrict segregation in the federal public service; as supervisor of the defense program he could reduce segregation among government contractors; as chief legislator he could use his prestige to support civil rights legislation; as chief executive he could nominate to federal positions men opposed to segregation. The strategists of the antisegregation interest elected to push hard here. The growth in the number of Negro voters and their movement to urban centers in the North made them an important part of the presidential constituency. The electoral college system enhanced the significance of this voting power. Furthermore, trade union leaders living in urban areas had become increasingly active against segregation.

6. Action by the Supreme and other federal courts? These judges could interpret the Constitution and federal statutes to label government-supported segregation unconstitutional and to expand federal protection of civil rights. A Supreme Court decision that segregation is unconstitutional would have a number of tactical advantages. The official ideology which places the Supreme Court outside of politics made it more likely that a Supreme Court ruling that segregation is unconstitutional would be more acceptable than a like decision by Congress that segregation is illegal. A Supreme Court ruling would be geographically more useful than a similar decision by state courts. Moreover, by the late 1930s the 1932 election had been translated into a shift in interest representation on the federal bench. Judicial power offered the best hope of success.

The desegregationists estimated the situation with great accuracy. No decision of the Supreme Court since 1935 has sustained the segregation interest, although it was not until 1954 that segregation in public schools was specifically declared unconstitutional.[24] But beginning in 1935 the Supreme Court majority has consistently moved toward desegregation. In that year the Court began to make it more difficult for state officials to exclude Negroes from juries.[25] In 1941 the justices started to label as unconstitutional every maneuver to restrict Negro voting.[26] In transportation, housing, trade union membership, and public education the justices attacked devices designed to exclude Negroes. Whether it be an alleged violation of the equal rights clause, due process clause, commerce clause, or Interstate Commerce Commission Act, federal judges under the Supreme Court's leadership have supported the claim of those working to destroy racial discrimination.[27]

The executive branch has also participated in the antisegregation interest. Congress refused to enact new civil rights legislation, but the Department of Justice and the Supreme Court have accomplished some of the goals by expanding the coverage and protection of the existing statutes.[28] Presidents have abolished segregation in the armed forces, established procedures to pressure government munitions contractors into employment on the basis of merit, and expanded opportunities for Negroes in federal service. It would serve no purpose for this essay to describe in detail all these activities or the scores of court cases. However, the story of the National Association for the Advancement of Colored People's attempt to win judicial support against discriminatory housing practices furnishes an interesting example of groups before the courts.

THE NAACP BEFORE THE COURTS[29] In 1917 the Supreme Court invalidated a Louisville ordinance requiring residential segregation, but in 1926 ruled that agreements among individuals to exclude Negroes from owning or using property could be enforced by state judges without violating the Constitution.[30] Consequently thousands of restrictive covenants were signed which excluded Negroes (and others) from a large portion of the desirable housing in the United States.

The National Association for the Advancement of Colored People went to work to reverse the 1926 decision. By 1945 the NAACP had made five applications for writs of certiorari in order to get the Supreme Court to reconsider the question. The Court either denied the petitions or sidestepped the constitutional issue.[31] In 1945 the Court denied certiorari again, but two justices specifically dissented from the refusal to review. It takes only four votes to grant the petition.

Each denial of the writ was a victory for the segregation interest since it left the 1926 decision undisturbed. The NAACP moved with caution. Their attorneys did not want to build up a record of denials. At the same time they wanted to keep up the pressures on the Supreme Court. By 1947 the NAACP officials felt that Justices Murphy and Rutledge were anxious to hear the issue, and only Justice Burton was definitely opposed. The next step was to find a case or cases which Murphy and Rutledge could use to persuade at least two of their colleagues to vote for certiorari.

Five cases, scattered throughout the nation, had been instituted in 1945. Each involved an attempt by whites to gain injunctions to keep Negroes from owning or living in houses covered by restrictive covenants. In each instance it was the white who had first invoked judicial authority. In each case the trial judge had issued the injunction. From the NAACP's point of view these cases would provide excellent ones to carry to the Supreme Court.

The NAACP furnished legal counsel for some and advice for the other Negro formal parties. The litigants on the other side also received organizational help. For example, Mrs. Kraemer, the party of record in St. Louis, who represented the segregation interest, was hesitant and expressed little desire to litigate. But the Marcus Avenue Improvement Association of property owners, with a judicious use of candy, flowers, and pep talks, persuaded Mrs. Kraemer to provide the "standing" necessary in order to contest the issue in the courts. Finally the Supreme Court granted petitions for certiorari to review three of the cases.

Meantime, the NAACP, perhaps remembering Professor Chafee's admonition that victories must first be won in the minds of men before they are won in the Courts (minds of judges), did its best to build up a body of legal opinion in support of its goal. The task of the NAACP was to overcome thirty years of adverse judicial precedents. They sought to do so by getting articles published in law reviews that were critical of the precedents and which stressed social and economic factors. Their success is measured by the over thirty books and articles which appeared between 1946 and 1948 urging the Supreme Court to reverse its 1926 decision. Only one article appeared in support of that decision.[32]

The NAACP did not fail to call the Supreme Court justices' attention to the law review articles as evidence of the general agreement among legal experts that the law should be changed. Nineteen organizations filed *amicus curiae* briefs to support the NAACP, including the Department of Justice which brought to the support of the desegregation interest the prestige and expertness of the executive branch. Five organizations entered briefs in opposition. Finally, the decision. The Supreme Court declared that the use of state judicial power to enforce racial restrictive covenants was unconstitutional.[33] The desegregation interests won a battle. However, the war continued.

LAISSEZ FAIRE AND THE SUPREME COURT   Although the NAACP is a well-organized interest representative, the conflicts in which it participates are no different from the many others which make up the business of the judiciary. Another struggle, viewed in somewhat broader terms, took place following the Civil War between those who wanted governmental regulation of some economic enterprises and those who felt that the government should leave these businesses alone. This is an oft told story and the details need not detain us here. But the broad sweep of the conflict may be instructive.

After the Civil War those working to industrialize the United States dominated the executive and legislative branches of the national government. Eventually they were also represented by the Supreme Court majority as well. But in some states the legislature spoke occasionally for other interests. Once in awhile so did Congress.

The industrialization of the United States increased conflicts between employers and employees, between producers of industrial products and their consumers. By and large, employers and producers opposed governmental regulation and insisted that wage rates, conditions of labor, and prices charged should be determined by the nongovernmentally regulated conduct of enterprisers. On the other hand, many employees and users of industrial commodities—especially railroad transportation —desire state and national governments to regulate prices charged, to decisions, are carried out in terms of certain verbal symbols. Interests unrepresented by the judges may seek to have the judicial decision reversed by Congress or some other agency, but they must attack the decision as "judicial legislation." As previously noted, according to the prevailing ideology, President, Congress, and other agencies should not interfere with the judges, especially if it appears that the interference is merely to please the majority. Such attempts to overcome an adverse judicial decision or to influence the judges are thought to destroy the independence of the courts and undermine our system of government of law and not of men. All agree upon this. But if the judges engage in judicial legislation or are swayed by personal or partisan biases, then it is permissible for Congress to set things right. Thus groups wanting Congress to interfere seek to have the offending decisions labeled as judicial legislation. Those who favor the decision are equally vehement in calling it sound law.

"JUDICIAL LEGISLATION" VERSUS "SOUND LAW" Before 1937, when federal judges represented the laissez-faire cluster of interests, the defeated groups accused the court majority of giving a tortured construction to the Constitution, of deciding cases according to their own economic predilections, and of forgetting the limits to their function.[5] The subjective element in the judges' choices was stressed and the anti-majoritarian aspect of judicial power was brought to public attention. Mechanical jurisprudence was attacked as a sham behind which judges legislated. On the other hand, the groups supported by the judicial majority accused the critics of misunderstanding the nature of the judicial function, of undermining our government, and of trying to destroy the independence of the courts. They argued that the judges were merely applying "the law" and should not be maligned by disappointed litigants.

Since 1937 the identity of the groups attacking or defending the decisions has altered, but the nature of the argument remains the same. For example, in 1950 Senator Bricker accused the Supreme Court, especially Justices Black, Douglas, Murphy, and Rutledge, of "resorting to some process of illegitimate statutory interpretation to reach a result coinciding with their own left wing attitudes and opinions."[6] The Senator warned, "Judicial legislation sooner or later must lock the Supreme Court and Congress in another open struggle for power. . . ." The Senator thought it unfair that whenever Congress has to correct "judicial legislation" it subjects "Congress to unwarranted, but perfectly natural criticism. The general public still assumes, almost instinctively, that the Supreme Court should be immune from criticism, because unlike Congress it is emotionally unconcerned about the desirability or undesirability of particular legislation."[7]

When the Supreme Court majority "courageously" agreed with the majority of Congress that President Truman had acted unconstitutionally in seizing the steel mills,[8] the approving Senators were quick with their praises for those justices who had arrived "at the conclusion that," to quote Senators Cain and Ferguson, "we have a government of laws and not of men." (Two years before Senator Ferguson had indicated his sympathy with Senator Bricker's attack on Justice Black, the justice who wrote the opinion for the Court in the steel seizure case, for engaging in "judicial legislation.") Senator George told his colleagues that the soundness of the majority opinions was recognized by "all Americans who are without undue prejudice" and he left no doubt into which category he placed the three dissenting justices.[9]

Other examples that it is "the American tradition . . . to denounce the Court when it adopts your opponent's views and applaud it when it subscribes to the Truth, i.e., your own position," could be readily collected.[10] Critical comments about Supreme Court decisions upholding national regulation of natural gas producers, sustaining application of antitrust laws to insurance companies, banning the base-point system in the cement industry, forbidding discrimination on interstate trains, or any other major decision could be gathered. In all of these comments, disapproving congressmen charged the judges with engaging in legislation. When the Supreme Court declared public-school segregation unconstitutional it let loose a torrent of criticism. As Professor John P. Roche wrote, "Southern politicians known far and wide as pillars of conservatism and the rule of law, are now attacking the 'political court.' It is predictable that, had the decisions gone the other way, they would be equally vigorous in their assault on any who criticized the determination of our 'great impartial tribunal.' Viewed *sub specie aeternitatis*, the basic principle of American constitutional interpretation, and of American politics, is 'whose ox is gored?' "[11]—in our terms, whose interest is supported.

CIRCUMVENTING JUDICIAL DECISIONS In addition to attaching disapproving labels to decisions, what are the alternatives for an interest working to overcome or minimize a judicial defeat?

1. The decision can be ignored and its enforcement opposed by force. Prior to the Civil War, especially during the early years, the federal judiciary did not have much popular support, its prestige was not high. Decisions were sometimes flouted. Today the interest opposed to the use of force is stronger than in the early years. It is unlikely that force will be used or that decisions will be openly ignored, at least by the formal parties to a lawsuit. Nevertheless, open defiance and refusal to comply with court rulings are not unknown. There is the same discrepancy between conduct and judicially developed rules that one finds between actual conduct and legislatively formulated rules. Some men still fail to report their incomes despite the commands of Congress and some policemen continue to use third-degree methods despite the pronouncements of the Supreme Court.

Not long ago the Texas State Land Commissioner announced that he would go to jail before turning over to the national government the more than $8,000,000 received as royalties from oil which the Supreme Court had decided did not belong to Texas.[12] In 1947 a House Committee recommended that no money be appropriated to meet the Supreme Court's judgment in *United States* v. *Lovett*[13] (but Congress did). Recently, a large number of southern officials announced that they will not permit the desegregation of public schools despite the Supreme Court's decision and that they will defy whatever orders the Court issues. However, the more normal procedures for disappointed interests is to use subtle methods rather than open defiance, to find legal means to avoid compliance.

Whether a judicial command is being violated is often debated. Yet it is clear that conduct is often continued after the Supreme Court has pronounced it illegal or unconstitutional. Those who carry on as before usually insist that they are complying with the Court's order and that they have altered their activity so that what they are continuing to do no longer comes within the ban of the Court's decisions. The Fifteenth Amendment, for example, declares that no person shall be deprived of the right to vote because of race, color, or previous condition of servitude. This Amendment became part of the Constitution in 1870. But in some places by one method or another Negroes were denied the right to vote by government officials. After the Supreme Court would strike down one procedure as unconstitutional, another would be tried. Whether this response to the decisions should be labeled defiance of the Court or given some other label can be left to the participants in the conflict. But the student of the judiciary should not blind himself to the significance of the activity frustrating the courts' rulings.

2. A defeated interest can seek to overcome a judicial ruling by a formal amendment to the Constitution. The amending procedures give advantages to interests opposing change. Nevertheless, the Eleventh, Fourteenth, and Sixteenth Amendments represent victories for interests which had failed to find the desired representation by judges.

3. A defeated interest can "appeal" from the courts to Congress. Even if the decision involves a constitutional question, Congress can reassert the interest previously struck down. Congress can interpret the decision narrowly. For example, in 1935, after the Supreme Court declared that the Agricultural Adjustment Act was unconstitutional, Congress achieved its goal of regulating production by use of another verbal formula.

Since 1937 the Supreme Court has only twice declared acts of Congress unconstitutional, but it has interpreted statutes to represent interests other than those which had the support of a majority of Congress. As a result Congress has frequently "reversed" the Court's interpretation of statutes. Among many examples the following can be mentioned: Congress extinguished claims for portal-to-portal pay after the Supreme

Court had allowed them; Congress rushed to support state fair-trade laws after a Supreme Court decision made them useless; Congress made unilateral interpretations of some contracts no longer binding upon businessmen after a Supreme Court decision held to the contrary; Congress removed immigration officials from the Administrative Procedures Act after the Supreme Court said that they were covered; Congress turned over to the states offshore oil after the Supreme Court decided that the national government had a paramount interest in this oil; the Taft-Hartley Act and the Immigration and Naturalization Act of 1954 contain many provisions aimed at restricting or reversing Supreme Court rulings; Congress amended the Fair Labor Standards Act to exclude from its coverage certain workers who judges had previously ruled were entitled to protection.

Of course not all interests defeated in the judicial forum are successful in the legislature. Many times the same interests are dominant in both the Congress and the Supreme Court. Moreover, congressional support to overcome a judicial decision does not necessarily insure victory. Interests adversely affected by the act of Congress can return to judges. For example, prior to 1914 federal judges used the antitrust laws to interfere with attempts by trade unions to organize unions. In 1914 Congress declared that labor should not be considered a commodity and the antitrust laws should not be applied to trade union activity. President Gompers of the American Federation of Labor hailed this provision as labor's Magna Carta. But within a short time the judges were interpreting the new statute to permit the same judicial interference with trade-union activity as before.

4. Defeated by the Supreme Court, the adversely affected interests can regain victory in the lower courts. The Supreme Court normally returns cases to trial judges via the intermediate appellate tribunals. It is these trial judges who have to interpret and apply the Supreme Court decisions, and they can do so in order to minimize the significance of their superior's orders. Between 1941 and 1951 out of 175 cases which the Supreme Court reversed and remanded to state tribunals there were forty-six cases involving further litigation. "In slightly less than half of these cases the party successful in the Supreme Court was unsuccessful in the state court following the remand."[14] Thus even for the immediate parties, a Supreme Court victory is not cause for too much celebration. As between the interests, Supreme Court victory for one hardly means that the other lost the war.

More significant than the state judges' treatment of cases remanded to them is their application and interpretation of doctrines announced by the Supreme Court which are supposed to bind all judges in future cases. But what a Supreme Court rule of law means depends on how other judges interpret that rule. And this interpretation is interest activity, understandable in terms of the group conflict. For example, in 1948 the

Supreme Court ruled that state judges should not issue injunctions to enforce racial restrictive covenants.[15] The next year the Missouri Supreme Court held that the federal Supreme Court had only ordered state judges not to issue injunctions, but had not forbidden state judges to entertain actions for damages.[16] Four year later the Supreme Court ruled that the Missouri judges had made the wrong decision.[17]

In 1880 the Supreme Court ruled that it was unconstitutional to exclude Negroes from juries.[18] But Negroes were not called to sit on juries. They were excluded by the practices of court officials. In many states the judges did not interfere. In 1935 the Supreme Court looked behind the formal regulations.[19] The justices said that long-continued absence of Negroes on juries in counties where there was a sizable Negro population presented a presumption of exclusion. In some southern states this Supreme Court decision was countered by placing a single Negro on a grand jury whenever a Negro was to be indicted. This too won the sanction of some state judges who concluded that such a practice did not violate the Constitution.[20] When it appeared that the Supreme Court might question this procedure, in some jurisdictions the state's attorney used his peremptory challenges to exclude Negroes from juries. Texas, Michigan, and inferior federal judges have held that this practice does not violate the Constitution. So far the Supreme Court has refused to review.[21] Texas judges also narrowly construed the Supreme Court's decisions and interpreted them so as not to forbid the systematic exclusion of Latin-Americans from juries. In 1954 the Supreme Court announced otherwise.[22]

The recent history of motion picture censorship provides another example of how some state judges have minimized the scope of a rule formulated by the Supreme Court. In 1952 the Supreme Court held that a state could not constitutionally refuse to license the showing of a picture, "The Miracle" because it was alleged to be "sacrilegious."[23] This standard, said the justices, was much too vague. The next year New York judges decided that the Supreme Court's ruling did not apply to pictures alleged to be "immoral" and Ohio judges sustained censorship of a film alleged to be "harmful."[24] The Supreme Court reversed. Then the Illinois supreme court sustained a ban on "The Miracle" because it was alleged to be obscene. The United States Supreme Court refused to review (by a vote of six to three).[25]

State judges do not always restrict the coverage of a Supreme Court doctrine. Sometimes they represent interests who want to expand the coverage of the doctrine and who use the Supreme Court decision to justify their rulings. Recently California judges declared state laws restricting marriage among members of different races and some of the alien land laws to be unconstitutional. Although the United States Supreme Court has not specifically held these kinds of laws to be unconstitutional, the California judges argued that the recent direction of high court opinions requires the offending state statutes to be struck down.[26] However, the action of the California judges is unusual. Apparently during the last several decades state judges have been more apt to minimize Supreme Court decisions than to expand their coverage.[27]

Subordinate federal judges also must construe commands of the Supreme Court. For example, two district judges recently ruled that the Supreme Court's school segregation decision does not extend to recreational facilities.[28] Both of these judges sit in states where segregation has long been established.

5. An interest unrepresented by a Supreme Court decision can work to get the Court itself to alter, ignore, or narrowly construe its previous command. A hostile critic of the present Supreme Court counted thirty-two decisions which he said had been reversed by the Court between 1931 and 1953.[29] Justice Douglas made a conservative count and discovered eighteen cases which clearly overruled previous decisions in the period 1860 to 1890 and sixteen such cases between 1937 and March 1949.[30]

Is the Constitution What the Judges Say It Is?

Most lawyers and political scientists make a fundamental distinction between judicial review and statutory interpretation. Professor David Truman, for example, writes: "Judicial interpretations of statutes . . . finality is not assured: the Congress or a State legislature may legitimately overrule the interpretation that a court has placed upon a legislative act. When an act has been declared unconstitutional, however, almost the only recourse, unless the court reverses itself, is the long, slow, and seldom traveled road of constitutional amendment."[31] In a limited sense, of course, this is true. The interest opposing a particular act certainly has an advantage if the judges have labeled the action unconstitutional, but it is certainly not a determinative advantage. *Judicial interpretation of the Constitution is not necessarily any more final than interpretation of a statute.*

The classic defense of judicial review is based on the argument that judges are not likely to be swayed by passion and prejudice whereas elected representatives are. Therefore, if judges check the momentary passions of the populace, in time the sober second thoughts and long-run interests will become apparent. Alexander Hamilton argued that an independent judiciary would protect the nation from "the effects of those ill-humors which the arts of designing men, or the influence of particular conjunctures, sometimes disseminate among the people themselves."[32] Mr. Harrison Tweed, President of the American Law Institute and past president of the American Bar Association, restated the classic position when he told a Senate subcommittee: "A crisis involving some great question of policy . . . as between Congress and the Supreme Court on a question of whether a given act is constitutional or not . . . would be a moment when consideration of a careful, deliberate and sound nature cannot be expected from Congress. . . . So it is to be expected that at such a moment as that, the constitutional judgment of the Supreme Court will be a far sounder, further forward-looking judgment, than anything that could be expected of Congress."[33]

Does the evidence support this argument? Have judges been better able to discern the long-run demands of the electorate, the people's sober second thoughts? On the contrary, the second thoughts—sober or not— seem to have been cast in favor of Congress. In almost every decision in which judges have imposed a check upon Congress in the name of the Constitution, in *one way or another* Congress eventually has done what the judges at first said it should not and could not do. Sometimes it took a constitutional amendment, sometimes a reversal by the judges, but in one way or another, Congress (that is, the interests represented by the congressional majority) did it.

The Supreme Court decided that Congress could not ban slavery within the territories; eight years later slavery was banned throughout the United States.[34] The Court told Congress that it could not make paper money legal tender; a year later Congress was still doing so and this time with the Court's blessings.[35] The Supreme Court decided that Congress could not levy a graduated income tax without apportioning it among the states according to population, but less than twenty years later Congress did so.[36] The Supreme Court told Congress that it could not regulate a company that controlled 95 per cent of sugar refining because this activity did not directly affect interstate commerce; a few years later Congress was allowed to regulate the business of buying livestock in the Chicago stockyards and today its regulations cover business trans-actions whose impact on interstate commerce is somewhat less than direct.[37] The Supreme Court said Congress could not tax salaries of state employees, but these employees now pay federal taxes.[38] The Supreme Court said that Congress could not ban the interstate shipment of goods produced by children; today it is a federal crime to hire children to produce goods which one intends to ship in interstate commerce.[39] The Court said that Congress could not regulate agricultural production; one year later Congress did so. In fact, it is difficult to find a major decision denying Congress authority to do something which it does not do today. Brooks Adams concluded, "No court can, because of the nature of its being, effectively check a popular majority acting through a coordinate legislative assembly. . . ."[40] It may be added that in the United States a boost from the President is helpful.

It is thus clear that the nine justices sitting on top of the federal court structure or even all the four hundred federal judges do not always determine with finality how interest conflicts shall be resolved. On the other hand, it is equally clear that the activity of these decision-makers has some impact on the outcome of the group struggle. Although the emphasis in this chapter has been upon the action of groups seeking to overcome an adverse court decision, groups whose interests are supported by the decision are often successful. To win judicial support is a strategically important step for any interest. It brings the prestige of the judges, their opinions, and their sanction to enforce desired policy. Many illustrations could be cited which indicate the importance of having the judges on your side, but the judges' side does not always win. A judicial decision is but one phase in the never-ending group conflict, a single facet of the political process.

Concluding Remarks

This concludes this brief survey of federal courts in the political process. What federal judges do, how they are organized to do it, and their organizational relations to other agencies of government and to other groups were described. Conflicts to control personnel of the courts and to influence decision-making were discussed, as well as the activity which follows a decision.

Generalizations about judicial activity that have been made must be considered tentative. Because many studies of courts are not cast in political terms, our knowledge about judicial participation in the political process is limited. We know little of the precise conditions under which judicial power is invoked, the factors which make for success, and the consequences which flow from judicial participation. What are the variables related to an increase in litigation, to a decrease? When is litigation chosen over legislation? What are the consequences of entrusting decisions to judges instead of legislators? Do state courts tend to represent different interests than federal courts? Under what conditions do Supreme Court decisions have a significant impact upon behavior?

Perhaps we can begin to answer such questions if—to restate the general theme once again and finally—courts are placed in a political framework and seen as a facet in the group struggle. At least the activity of judges can be placed in the same descriptive system now being used to describe legislative and administrative behavior. Those concerned with analysis of the policy-making process will no longer have to ignore judicial action or alter their system of description when discussing the judiciary. The political scientist can then develop a political science of the judicial process without encroaching on the special reserves of the historian, the lawyer, or the psychologist.

Footnotes to the Study

Chapter One

1. Bertram M. Gross: *The Legislative Struggle*, New York, McGraw-Hill Book Company, 1953.
2. No attempt will be made here to defend or explore the epistemological or methodological arguments to support this orientation, but the reader is referred to the following works: A. F. Bentley: *The Process of Government*, Bloomington, Ind., Principia Press, 1949 (reissue); David B. Truman: *The Governmental Process*, New York, Alfred A. Knopf, Inc., 1951, especially Chapter 15; Charles B. Hagan: "The Group in a Political Science," paper prepared for conference, "A Search for the Relevant Political Concepts," Northwestern University, June 15–19, 1954; Earl Latham: "The Group Basis of Politics: Notes for a Theory," *American Political Science Review* 46: 376–97 (June 1952); Phillip Monypenny: "Political Science and the Study of Groups: Notes to Guide a Research Project," *The Western Political Quarterly* 7: 183–201 (June 1954); Richard Taylor: "Arthur F. Bentley's Political Science," *Western Political Quarterly* 5: 214–30 (June 1952); Dorwin Cartwright (ed.): *Field Theory in Social Science*, New York, Harper & Brothers, 1951, especially contributions of Kurt Lewin; John Dewey: *Human Nature and Conduct*, New York, The Modern Library, 1930.
3. Human activity is so interrelated that to abstract an action from the continuous stream and place it into a single interest category is always arbitrary. A particular act can always be assigned to several interests. It depends in part upon the observer's perspective, especially upon the time period he is considering.
4. Motives of actors and internal thought process are excluded from this inquiry. Our data will be what people write, say, and do. Their "mind-stuff" is left to their biographers and psychoanalysts. As Brooks Adams wrote when discussing President Grant's appointments to the Supreme Court and the Court's subsequent reversal of its Legal Tender decisions: "To me it is immaterial whether General Grant and Mr. Hoare did or did not nominate judges with a view to obtaining a particular judgment. I am concerned not with what men thought, but with what they did, and with the effect of their acts at the moment, upon their fellow citizens." Brooks Adams: *The Theory of Social Revolutions*, New York, The Macmillan Company, 1913, pp. 153–54.
5. The persistence after so many years of the notion that men can raise themselves up by their intellectual bootstraps and substitute an externalized

"law" for human choice-making, raises the presumption that this fiction serves a basic purpose and a deep-felt human need. Judge Jerome Frank's suggestion that it serves for adults the same purpose as the father image for children is well known (see his *Law and the Modern Mind,* New York, Coward-McCann, 1930). Max Rumelin, a German jurist, suggests: "Jurists are inclined to be afraid of value judgments, which are always colored with a certain amount of subjectivity; at least they are loath to pronounce such evaluations openly, since they invite the criticism of the interested parties or groups to a much higher degree than do genuinely or apparently logical deductions." (*The Jurisprudence of Interests,* Cambridge, Harvard University Press, 1948, p. 14.) Perhaps the fiction makes judicial decisions enforceable and more acceptable to defeated interests. The judgments become not those of fallible men, but the inexorable command of the "law."

The rejection here of law as an external reality outside of and independent of human beings is entirely different from and not to be confused with the rejection of right and wrong, nor is it to be confused with any rejection of the command, will, or reason of God.

6. No attempt will be made to add to the existing definitions of "law." Terms such as "constitution," "statutes," "judicial decision," "sanctions," "rules of behavior" will be used whenever it is important to have a specific referent.

7. Victor G. Rosenblum's *Law as a Political Instrument,* New York, Random House, Inc., 1955, another of the Short Studies in Political Science, presents several detailed case studies of judicial policy-making and explores its implications for democratic theory.

Chapter Two

1. "Illegal" is used here in a broader sense than "criminal." In a civil case where A sues B for negligence, the decision that the law requires B to pay A damages is a decision that when men act as B did, they act illegally and should pay damages. The activity is illegal in the sense that judges will use their authority to penalize the conduct. If the activity in question is that of public officials, judges may label it unconstitutional. But judicial activity is of the same order whether it is a decision that a firm violated the Sherman Act or the sheriff violated the Fourteenth Amendment. Both decisions are interest activity. However, the consequence of a pronouncement that a sheriff has acted unconstitutionally may be different from a pronouncement that he has acted illegally. For one thing, it is probably more difficult to overcome an adverse constitutional decision. In addition, the response to a judicial labeling of conduct as unconstitutional is probably different from the response to a judicial declaration of illegality.

2. Frederick V. Cahill, Jr.: *Judicial Legislation,* New York, The Ronald Press Company, 1952, p. 152.

3. *Olmstead* v. *United States,* 277 U.S. 438 (1928), dissenting opinion, at 470. *Congressional Record* 100: 461 ff. (April 8, 1954).

4. Professor Zechariah Chafee noted the important interrelations among judicial opinions, nonjudicial behavior, and judicial decisions when he commented: "The victories of liberty of speech must be won in the mind before

they are won in the Courts. In that battlefield of reason we possessed in 1925 new and powerful weapons, the dissenting opinions of Justices Holmes and Brandeis. . . ." *Free Speech in the United States,* Cambridge, Mass., Harvard University Press, 1948, p. 325.

5. As used here and throughout this essay, "power" is not conceived of as a thing, but is an observation and prediction about a set of interrelated actions. To say that Congress has the power to tax is a short-hand way to predict on the basis of past observation that if congressmen go through certain procedures, then other men will act in such and such a way and money will be received from some men and deposited in the public treasury. Likewise, to say that judges do not have the power to levy taxes is to observe that they are not recognized to have this function and to predict that if they tried to do so other men would react in such and such a way and that taxes would not be collected. Since it is too clumsy to spell all this out with each term, it will be used henceforth without further explanation or apology. Note that as used in this manner the term "power" combines both the factor of recognition of the rightfulness of the action and a prediction as to the ability to accomplish the objective.

6. The doctrine of finality is applied only to courts created by Congress to decide cases of the kind mentioned in Article III of the Constitution. These "constitutional courts" are to exercise only judicial power. Congress may establish agencies, call them courts, and give judges of these "legislative courts" authority which is not recognized as "judicial" and which would not be proper for judges under Article III.

7. *Hayburn's Case,* 2 Dall. 409 (1792).

8. Quoted by Andrew C. McLaughlin: *A Constitutional History of the United States,* New York, D. Appleton-Century Company, 1935, pp. 581–82.

9. 332 U.S. 19 (1947).

10. It is interesting to note that Congress has "clothed the admission of aliens to citizenship in the mantle of a case" in order to give the appearance of an adversary proceeding. Thus judges perform this function and the judicial conscience is apparently soothed sufficiently that the judges can continue to insist that federal judges of constitutional courts will not undertake "administrative duties." Similarly, the judges of the Court of Claims, which Congress recently decided should be considered a constitutional court have indicated that despite their new statute they will continue to act on cases referred to them by Congress. See *Congressional Record* **99**: 8943–45 (July 16, 1953).

11. *Luther* v. *Borden,* 7 How. 1. (1849).

12. *Field* v. *Clark,* 143 U.S. 649 (1892); *Coleman* v. *Miller,* 307 U.S. 433 (1939).

13. *Foster* v. *Neilson,* 2 Pet. 253 (1829); *Commercial Trust Co. of New Jersey* v. *Miller,* 262 U.S. 51 (1923).

14. *Colegrove* v. *Green,* 328 U.S. 549 (1946).

15. *Luther* v. *Borden.*

16. *Coleman* v. *Miller.*

17. 328 U.S. 549 (1946).

18. *Colegrove* v. *Green,* to mention one of the more obvious.

19. *South* v. *Peters,* 339 U.S. 276 (1950).

20. The Constitution delimits the judicial power of the United States to cover the following kinds of cases: (1) those in which a state is a party (but not those initiated by individuals or foreign governments against a state); (2) those in which the United States is a party; (3) those which affect representatives of foreign nations; (4) those between citizens of two or more states; (5) those arising under the Constitution, federal law, or treaty; (6) those arising out of a land dispute in which the land is claimed on the basis of grants of two or more states; (7) those arising under admiralty and maritime jurisdiction.

21. Since 1937, when the Supreme Court stopped representing the interests of businessmen, the businessmen and their legal allies stopped supporting the justices. They began to pine for the old days and to accuse the Roosevelt- and Truman-appointed justices of being poor lawyers and biased politicians. At the same time, the interests these judges have represented have failed to come to their rescue. These were the groups who in the past had been skeptical of judicial power. Although it was being used to support some of their values, these "liberals" did not give the liberal justices the same kind of support that the "conservatives" formerly gave to the conservative justices.

    Despite the lack of representation, the traditional defenders of federal judges, except possibly some southern Democrats, have not abandoned their support of federal courts. Apparently the traditional defenders believe that over the long run the interests they favor are more likely to be supported by judges than by legislators or administrators. Inferior federal judges, from their perspective, continue to represent the "right" interests and they attribute their disappointment with the Supreme Court to the partisanship of Roosevelt and Truman. But for whatever reasons, the conservative supporters of federal judicial power have remained steadfast. See *Congressional Record* 100: 6340–47 (May 11, 1954), and Commission on Organization of The Executive Branch of the Government, Task Force on Legal Services and Procedure, *Report on Legal Services and Procedures,* March, 1955.

22. *Congressional Record* 101: 1152–53 (Feb. 9, 1955) (Daily Edition).

23. 16 Pet. 1 (1842).

24. *Louisville, Cincinnati, and Charleston R. Co.* v. *Letson,* 2 How. 497 (1844).

25. See Mitchell Wendell: *Relations Between the Federal and State Courts,* New York, Columbia University Press, 1949, pp. 72–91.

26. See *Black and White Taxicab and Transfer Co.* v. *Case,* 276 U.S. 518 (1928).

27. "New Light on the History of the Federal Judiciary Act of 1789," *Harvard Law Review* 29: 81–88 (1923).

28. 293 U.S. 335 (1934).

29. H.R. Rep. No. 1506, 82 Cong., 1st Session.

30. Concurring in *Lumberman's Mutual Casualty Company* v. *Florence R. Elbert,* 348 U.S. 48, 58 (1955).

31. *Ibid.,* p. 57.

32. Joseph C. Hutcheson, Jr.: "The Natural Law and the Right to Property," *Notre Dame Lawyer* 26: 645 (1951).

33. *Ibid.,* p. 642.
34. See unsigned article, "Joseph C. Hutcheson, Jr., Chief Judge, Fifth Circuit Court of Appeals," *American Bar Association Journal* 35: 546 ff. (July 1949).
35. *National Labor Relations Board* v. *Waterman Steamship Co.,* 309 U.S. 206 (1940).
36. "Joseph C. Hutcheson, Jr.", *op. cit.,* p. 615.
37. *United States* v. *Paramount Pictures,* 334 U.S. 131 (1948).
38. *Mutual Film Corp.* v. *Industrial Commission of Ohio,* 236 U.S. 230 (1915).
39. *RD-DR Corp. and Film Classics Inc.* v. *Smith,* 183 F 2d 562 (1950).
40. See Simon Rosenzweiz: "The Opinions of Judge Edgerton—A Study In the Judicial Process," *Cornell Law Quarterly* 37: 149–205 (1952). Mr. Rosenzweiz points out that as of 1952 there was a 60 per cent chance that the Supreme Court would review a decision of the Court of Appeals when Edgerton dissented as compared with a 13 per cent chance when he voted with the majority.
41. *Carr* v. *Corning,* 182 F 2d 14, 32–33 (1950); *Mays* v. *Burgess,* 147 F 2d 869 (1945); 152 F 2d 123 (1945).
42. *Baily* v. *Richardson,* 182 F 2d 46 (1950).
43. *Barsky* v. *United States,* 167 F 2d 241, 252 (1948).
44. See Note, "The Insubstantial Federal Question," *Harvard Law Review* **62**: 488 (1949).
45. Supreme Court Rules 19 (1).
46. See Robert L. Stern: "Denial of Certiorari Despite a Conflict," *Harvard Law Review* **66**: 468 (1953). See also series of four articles by Fowler V. Harper and associates which have appeared in volumes 99, 100, 101 and 102 of *University of Pennsylvania Law Review* entitled "What the Supreme Court Did Not Do in the 1949 [1950] [1951] [1952] Term."
47. Simon E. Sobeloff: "Attorney for the Government," *American Bar Association Journal* **41**: 232 (March 1955).

Chapter Three

1. Congress has used this authority to influence judicial decision-making, and some would amend the Constitution in order to prevent this by fixing the size of the Supreme Court at nine, and denying Congress authority to interfere with the Supreme Court's appellate jurisdiction over cases arising under the Constitution. (See *Composition and Jurisdiction of the Supreme Court,* Hearing before a Subcommittee of the Committee on the Judiciary, United States Senate, 83 Cong., 2d Sess., Jan. 29, 1954, pp. 2–3.) The Senate approved such an amendment but the House Judiciary Committee tabled it. The proponents of the amendment argued that it was necessary to close these constitutional loopholes which would permit Congress and President to interfere with the judiciary because "wherever courts suffer an invasion of their independence, law ends." Four days after the Senate voted approval, the Supreme Court declared public-school segregation unconstitutional. Thereupon some southerners introduced legislation to deprive the federal judges of authority to hear cases involving public

schools and they argued that Congress's control over Supreme Court jurisdiction was "firmly entrenched in our legal jurisprudence."

2. See Philbrick McCoy: "Judicial Selection and Judicial Conduct, A Preliminary Report of the Survey of the Legal Profession," *Southern California Law Review* 24: 1–41 (Dec. 1950).

3. Canon 28 of the Canons of Judicial Ethics adopted by the American Bar Association in 1924 and amended in 1933 reads in part as follows: "While entitled to entertain his personal views of political questions, and while not required to surrender his rights or opinions as a citizen, it is inevitable that suspicion of being warped by political bias will attach to a judge who becomes the active promoter of the interests of one political party as against another." Although the Canon makes some exceptions for judges elected to office on a party ticket, it concludes with the injunction that judges should not "engage generally in partisan activities."

4. Maxine B. Virtue (ed.): *Judge Medina Speaks,* Albany, Matthew Bender & Company, 1954, p. 53. In addition to identification with partisan causes, judges have to remain aloof from business and social connections which might appear to put them under obligation. See Canons and also Reports of the Task Forces of the Commission on Judicial and Congressional Salaries, *Judicial and Congressional Salaries,* 83 Cong. 2d Sess., Senate Document 97, Feb. 8, 1954, p. 35.

5. Canon 20: "A judge should be mindful that his duty is the application of general law to particular instances. . . ."

6. Canon 14: "A judge should not be swayed by partisan demands, public clamor or consideration of personal popularity or notoriety, nor be apprehensive of unjust criticism. . . ."

7. Canon 30 enjoins a state judge who gains office by popular election "not to announce his conclusions of law on disputed issues to secure class support." As we shall presently note, judicial nominees have frequently refused to comment before the Senate Judiciary Committee about their views on issues which they might possibly have to decide as judges if confirmed.

8. Feb. 11, 1955 quoted in *Congressional Record* 101: 882 (Feb. 14, 1955). Like all rules, the mores are at times ignored. Senator Ferguson and other members of the Senate closely questioned Judge McGranery and made him defend some of his decisions when they were considering his nomination to be Attorney General. Senate Judiciary Committee: *Hearings, Nomination of James P. McGranery,* 82 Cong. 2d Sess., May 5, 6, 7, 8, 1952, pp. 2–144.

9. See David B. Truman: *The Governmental Process,* New York, Alfred A. Knopf, Inc., 1951, 482–89.

10. Virtue, *op. cit.,* p. 215.

11. Fowler Harper and Edwin D. Etherington: "Lobbyists Before the Court," *Pennsylvania University Law Review* 101: 1173 (1953).

12. *Bridges* v. *California,* 314 U.S. 252 (1941). In 1947 the Court majority held that it was unconstitutional for a judge to punish for contempt those who made severe criticism of an elected judge's decision and made veiled threats of how the judge would fare at the next election. Justice Jackson dissented. He commented that it was easy for federal judges protected by elaborate safeguards to tell local elected judges to have fortitude in the

face of criticism, and he wrote: "Of course, the blasts of these little papers in this small community do not jolt us, but I am not so confident that we would be indifferent if a news monopoly in our entire jurisdiction should perpetrate this kind of attack on us." Earlier Jackson had observed: "I do not know whether it is the view of the Court that a judge must be thick-skinned or just thickheaded, but nothing in my experience or observation confirms the idea that he is insensitive to publicity." *Craig* v. *Harney*, 331 U.S. 367, 396, 397 (1947).

13. Judge Medina commented upon all the publicity he received as a result of presiding over Dennis case, "I was a mere symbol. . . . The people of America love their judges; they honor and revere them. . . ." Virtue, *op. cit.*, p. 5.

14. *Congressional Record* 94: 5132 (April 30, 1948). However, congressmen are not always so restrained. As Dennis Brogan has pointed out, "This admiration of the Courts is compatible with severe criticism of specific judges and judgments, but it seldom leads to criticism of the legal approach to the questions debated." D. W. Brogan: *Politics in America*, New York, Harper & Brothers, 1955, p. 400, n. 1.

15. *Congressional Record* 97: 8661 (July 23, 1951).

16. Davis of Georgia, *Congressional Record* 99: 6880 ff. (June 18, 1953).

17. Forrester of Georgia, *Ibid.*

18. *Composition and Jurisdiction of the Supreme Court,* Hearing before Subcommittee of the Committee on the Judiciary, Senate, 83 Cong., 2d Sess., Jan. 29, 1954, p. 9.

19. Some consider it a violation of ethics for other than bar associations to invite judges to banquets. See Henry Drinker: *Legal Ethics*, New York, Columbia University Press, 1953, p. 71.

20. It is interesting to note the close relation between defense of Justice Frankfurter and membership on the Harvard Law School Faculty, and criticism of Justice Frankfurter and membership on the Yale Law School Faculty. For example, Professor Walton Hamilton of Yale: "Mr. Justice Frankfurter has no feel for the dominant issues. . . . He does the best he can, often very well indeed, with the techniques in which he is proficient; it is a calamity that his skills happen to be petty skills. He is the victim of a bad legal education. . . ." *Yale Law Review* 56: 1460 (1947). Professor Fred Rodell of Yale in a review of Charles P. Curtis, Jr.'s *Lions Under the Throne* (Boston, Houghton Mifflin Co., 1947) which appeared in *Yale Law Review,* **56,** "I have no quarrel with Mr. Curtis choosing a hero for the Court; my quarrel is with his choice. For his choice is Justice Felix Frankfurter. Curtis is a Bostonian and a Harvard Law Graduate." Commenting on Harvard Professor Thomas Reed Powell's defense of Frankfurter, Rodell wrote: "Professor Thomas Reed Powell, Justice Frankfurter's official apologist in the law reviews . . . [writes] interminable 'concurring opinions' in the *Harvard Law Review*" whereas Yaleman Rodell said that Harvard historian Arthur Schlesinger, Jr. "created a convenient but cock-eyed dichotomy in *Fortune*" in defense of Frankfurter (*Ibid.*, pp. 1464–66). Harvard-man Paul A. Freund (*On Understanding the Supreme Court,* Boston, Little, Brown and Company, 1950) is sympathetic to Frankfurter. On the other hand Yaleman John P. Frank likes Yaleman Douglas and finds non-

Harvard Black to his liking. See his "Review and Basic Liberties" in Edmond Cahn (ed.): *Supreme Court and Supreme Law,* Bloomington, Indiana University Press, 1954, pp. 109 ff.

21. Brooks Adams: *The Theory of Social Revolutions,* New York, The Macmillan Company, 1913, p. 97.
22. Earl Latham: "The Supreme Court and The Supreme People," *The Journal of Politics* 16: 209 (1954).
23. In many states judges and legislators are elected for relatively short terms. It is difficult to generalize with confidence, but it does not appear that the method of selection is a significant factor in determining the interests represented by judges. The differences which structure the ways groups approach legislators and judges, remains about the same whether judges are elected or appointed. See Willard Hurst: *The Growth of American Law,* Boston, Little, Brown and Company, 1950, pp. 138 ff.
24. Both are quoted by H. C. Pritchett: *Civil Liberties and the Vinson Court,* Chicago, University of Chicago Press, 1954, p. 189.
25. American Bar Association: *Reports,* 1892, p. 213; cited by Benjamin F. Twiss: *Lawyers and the Constitution,* Princeton, Princeton University Press, 1942, p. 149.
26. Albert P. Blaustein and Charles O. Porter: *The American Lawyer: A Summary of the Survey of the Legal Profession,* Chicago, University of Chicago Press, 1954, p. 36.
27. Blaustein and Porter, *op. cit.*
28. *Congressional Record* 99: 634–35 (Jan. 22, 1954). Similarly when the charge was made that Mr. Walter Lippman was against the amendment, Senator Bricker responded, "I do not know that he is a lawyer or a constitutional authority." *Ibid.,* p. 637.
29. *Ibid.,* p. 657.
30. *Ibid.,* p. 638. See also Blaustein and Porter, *op. cit.,* p. 99.
31. Twiss, *op. cit.,* and Clyde E. Jacobs: *Law Writers and the Courts,* Berkeley, University of California Press, 1954.
32. *Yale Law Journal* 56: 1460 (1947).
33. Found in C. E. Vose: "NAACP Strategy in the Covenant Cases," *Western Reserve Law Review* 6: 118 (1955) from Foreword to *Yale Law Journal* 50: 737 (1941).
34. Clement E. Vose: "The Impact of Pressure Groups on Constitutional Interpretation," paper delivered at annual convention, American Political Science Association, Chicago, Illinois, Sept. 8, 1954; see also article mentioned above.

In addition to the 1937 constitutional revolution, the law reviews soundly criticized the 1940 Minnersville decision which was reversed by the Court in 1943 (see Francis H. Heller: "A Turning Point for Religious Liberty," *Virginia Law Review* 29: 450–53 (Jan. 1943) for evidence of law-review disapproval, disapproval which was brought to the Court's attention in the briefs filed in 1943). The law reviews also anticipated and called for *O'Malley* v. *Woodrough,* 307 U.S. 277 (1938) overruling *Evans* v. *Gore,* 253 U.S. 245 (1920) and *Girouard* v. *United States,* 319 U.S. 61 (1946) overruling 1929 and 1931 decisions. The reviews have also led the way in developing doctrines to extend the coverage of federal civil rights legislation and for restricting restrictive covenants and segregation. Other examples could be cited. On the other hand, the Supreme Court represents different values in its decisions interpreting the naturalization laws and rights of persons to counsel in state criminal cases than do the bulk of law-review writers.

However, before any generalizations can be made with any degree of confidence about correlations between law-review "decisions" and those of judges, more systematic research is needed.

35. Drawn in large part from James Willard Hurst: *The Growth of American Law*, Boston, Little, Brown and Company, 1950, pp. 363–64.
36. See Simon E. Sobeloff: "Attorney for the Government," *American Bar Association Journal* 41: 232 (March 1955) and Homer Cummings and Carl McFarland: *Federal Justice*, New York, The Macmillan Company, 1937.
37. *Nomination of Ernest A. Tolin*, Hearings before the Committee on the Judiciary, United States Senate, 82 Cong., 2d Sess., April 17, 1952, p. 17. p. 17.

Chapter Four

1. Mr. Ben R. Miller, a member of the American Bar Associations Committee on the Federal Judiciary, is concerned. He writes: "The danger is that if the lay public begins to realize these political facts of life their confidence in our courts may well wane. . . ." "Federal Judicial Appointments," *American Bar Association Journal* 41: 126 (Feb. 1955). Perhaps this fear of what the lay public may do helps to account for many lawyers' insistence that courts are not in politics, despite so much evidence to the contrary.
2. Brooks Adams wrote: "So long as the power to enact laws shall hinge on the complexion of benches of judges, so long will the ability to control a majority of the bench be as crucial a political necessity as the ability to control a majority in avowedly representative assemblies." *The Theory of Social Revolutions*, New York, The Macmillan Company, 1913, p. 54. But Adams thought that if judges were denied authority to declare acts of the Congress unconstitutional then groups would be indifferent to the judiciary. He failed to recognize the political nature of statutory interpretation and of the other phases of judicial activity besides judicial review.
3. Justice Frankfurter told the Senate Judiciary Committee which was conducting the hearing on his nomination to the Supreme Court, "It would be improper for a nominee no less than a member of the Court to express his personal views on controversial issues before the Court." U.S. Senate Subcommittee of the Committee on the Judiciary, Hearings, *Nomination of Felix Frankfurter*, 76 Cong., 1st Sess. (1939), p. 107.
4. Statistics up to 1944 compiled by the late Chief Judge Evan A. Evans and given in address to Legal Club of Chicago, February 14, 1944 and quoted by Ben R. Miller: "Federal Judicial Appointments: The Continuing Struggle for Good Judges," *American Bar Association Journal* 41: 125–28 (Feb. 1955).
5. See *Nomination of Ernest A. Tolin*, Hearings before Committee on the Judiciary, United States Senate, 82 Cong., 2d Sess., p. 3, April 17, 1952, and Miller, *op. cit.*, for description of these procedures.

6. Canon 2.
7. In March 1937, 70 per cent of those who responded to an American Institute of Public Opinion poll indicated that they would not favor the appointment of a nonlawyer to the Supreme Court.
8. For example, of forty-nine men who were confirmed by the Senate during the last three years of Truman's administration, the ABA Committee on Federal Judiciary had affirmatively recommended eighteen, thirteen of whom this Committee had considered outstanding. Of five men the Senate did not confirm, three had been opposed by the committee.
9. *Nomination of Ernest A. Tolin*, Hearings before the Committee on the Judiciary, United States Senate, 82 Cong., 2d Sess., April 17, 1952, p. 35.
10. Joseph P. Harris: *The Advice and Consent of the Senate*, Berkeley, University of California Press, 1953, p. 324.
11. Most of the materials in this section are drawn from Professor Harris's useful volume cited directly above.
12. "The people demand" or "the people believe" provides support for a group's position in about the same way as does "the law requires." The former appeals to the democratic credo, the latter to the constitutional.
13. *United Mine Workers* v. *Red Jacket Consolidated Coal and Coke Co.*, 18 F 839 (1927).
14. *Hitchman Coal and Coke Company* v. *Mitchell*, 245 U.S. 229 (1917).
15. Between 1928 and 1948 there have been only three judges of state courts of appellate and general jurisdiction to be impeached. In all three cases the defense won. Nor have other provisions for removing state judges been used. Albert P. Blaustein and Charles O. Porter: *The American Lawyer: A Summary of the Survey of the Legal Profession*, Chicago, University of Chicago Press, 1954, pp. 267–68.
16. *Congressional Record* 95: 14134 (Oct. 10, 1949).
17. *Congressional Record* 95: 9713–23 (July 18, 1949).
18. *Ibid.*, 96: 13443–45 (August 25, 1950). In contrast, when Hiss was convicted Representative Jackson of California gave to Judge Henry W. Goodard who presided over this successful conviction the "Congratulations and thanks of all America . . ." *Congressional Record* 96: 843 (Jan. 24, 1950).
19. *Ibid.*, 99: 6760 (June 17, 1953).
20. Quoted by Carl B. Swisher: *Roger B. Taney*, New York, The Macmillan Company, 1935, p. 573.
21. Charles Fairman: *Mr. Justice Miller and the Supreme Court, 1862–1890*, Cambridge, Harvard University Press, 1939, p. 379.
22. Letter to Horace Taft, Nov. 14, 1929, quoted by H. F. Pringle: *The Life and Times of William Howard Taft*, New York, Farrar & Rinehart, Inc., 1939, Vol. II, p. 967.
23. A judge who retires may be called back to duty. He cannot engage in any other business, but he draws the same salary as judges in active service and thus benefits from any raise. A judge who resigns on full pay continues to receive salary of the amount he was paid at the time of resignation, but he is no longer a judge and may participate in business and political affairs without the usual restraints.

24. The material in this section is taken from Felix Frankfurter and James M. Landis: *The Business of the Supreme Court,* New York, The Macmillan Company, 1928.
25. *Procter & Gamble Co.* v. *United States,* 225 U.S. 282 (1912).
26. *Hepburn* v. *Griswold,* 8 Wallace 603 (1870).
27. See Sidney Ratner: "Was the Supreme Court Packed by President Grant?" *Political Science Quarterly* **50**: 342–56 (1935).
28. *Knox* v. *Lee* (*Legal Tender Cases*), 12 Wallace, 457 (1871).
29. Catherine Sullivan Grigoroff: "A Study of the Political Strategy and Techniques Employed in the Court Reorganization Fight of 1937," unpublished master's thesis, University of Illinois, 1949.
30. *Congressional Record* **100**: 6340–47 (May 11, 1954); *New York Times,* Aug. 4, 1954.

Chapter Five

1. 322 U.S. 533 (1944).
2. See Phillip L. Sirotkin: "An Analysis of Congressional Attitudes Toward Supreme Court Decisions," unpublished doctoral dissertation, University of Chicago, 1951, which contains detailed case studies of congressional response both to the Southeastern Underwriters and tidelands oil decisions.
3. Mr. Loren Miller, attorney for the National Association for the Advancement of Colored People, observed in a letter to Professor Vose: " . . . Supreme Court cases involving larger issues are contests between opposing forces rather than law suits between individuals. They are cast as individual pieces of litigation because the Constitution guarantees the rights of individuals rather than those of groups. However, as a practical matter, the individual is unable to pursue his rights to the ultimate and hence the job is done by groups of people who find themselves situated as the individual is situated and who secure their own rights by securing the rights of the similarly situated individual."
4. *Smith* v. *Allwright,* 321 U.S. 649 (1944). When no activity can be discovered outside the courtroom which the observer can relate to the controversy between the formal parties in any direct sense, it is most likely that the case involves an interest widely supported and not controverted. For example, in a murder trial it is unlikely that the defendant will represent a larger promurdering interest.
5. Judicial procedure can be outlined according to the following steps: (1) determination of what court, if any, will accept jurisdiction—jurisdiction; (2) determination of who may bring the action—parties; (3) determination of where suit may be brought—venue; (4) determination of what process should be used to bring defendant or his property into court—process; (5) determination of relief to be sought—remedies; (6) determination of how the issue should be formulated—pleading; (7) pretrial procedures; (8) introduction of evidence and argument—trial; (9) decision and explanation by judges and/or jury; (10) review of decision by appellate judges; (11) enforcement of decision.
6. *Coleman* v. *Miller,* 307 U.S. 433 (1939).

7. See Robert K. Carr: *Quest for a Sword*, Ithaca, Cornell University Press, 1947.
8. See Fowler V. Harper and Edwin D. Etherington: "Lobbyists Before the Court," *Pennsylvania University Law Review* **101**: 1173 ff. (1953).
9. Supreme Court Rule 42 (1954). Justice Black dissented. He wrote: "Most of the cases before the Court involve matters that affect more people than the immediate record parties. I think the public interest would be better served by relaxing rather than tightening the rule against *amicus curiae* briefs." 98 L. ed. p. 1158 (1954).
10. *Pollock* v. *Farmers Loan & Trust Co.*, 157 U.S. 429 (1895).
11. *Carter* v. *Carter Coal Company*, 298 U.S. 238 (1936).
12. *Barrows* v. *Jackson*, 346 U.S. 249 (1953).
13. *Dred Scott* v. *Sandford*, 19 Howard 393 (1857); *Marbury* v. *Madison*, 1 Cranch 137 (1803). Many other cases of like nature could be cited.
14. *Schecter Poultry Corporation* v. *United States*, 295 U.S. 485 (1935).
15. *National Labor Relations Board* v. *Jones & Laughlin Steel Corp.*, 301 U.S. 1 (1937).
16. *National Labor Relations Board* v. *Friedman-Harry Marks Clothing Co.*, 301 U.S. 58 (1937).
17. This and the following section are drawn from Paul A. Freund: *On Understanding the Supreme Court*, Boston, Little, Brown & Co., 1950, pp. 92–116.
18. *Ashwander* v. *TVA*, 297 U.S. 288 (1936).
19. *Tennessee Electric Power Co.* v. *TVA*, 306 U.S. 118 (1939).
20. *Electric Bond and Share Company* v. *Securities Exchange Commission*, 303 U.S. 419 (1938).
21. *Civil Rights Cases*, 109 U.S. 3 (1883) and *United States* v. *Cruikshank*, 92 U.S. 542 (1875), for example. See also Morroe Berger: *Equality by Statute*, New York, Columbia University Press, 1952.
22. *Plessy* v. *Ferguson*, 163 U.S. 537 (1896).
23. Justice Harlan. It is interesting to note that when Justice Harlan's grandson was nominated by President Eisenhower to the Supreme Court, most of the votes against his nomination were from southerners.
24. *School Segregation Cases*, 347 U.S. 483 (1954).
25. *Norris* v. *Alabama*, 294 U.S. 587 (1935).
26. *United States* v. *Classic*, 313 U.S. 299 (1941); *Smith* v. *Allwright*, 321 U.S. 649 (1944); *Rice* v. *Elmore*, 165 F 2d 387 (1947); *Brown* v. *Baskin*, 78 F Supp. 933 (1948); *Terry* v. *Adams*, 345 U.S. 461 (1953), for examples.
27. For example, *Shelley* v. *Kraemer*, 334 U.S. 1 (1948); *Morgan* v. *Virginia*, 328 U.S. 373 (1946); *Henderson* v. *United States*, 339 U.S. 816 (1950); *Brotherhood of Railroad Trainmen* v. *Howard*, 343 U.S. (1952).
28. *Williams* v. *United States*, 341 U.S. 97 (1951), for example.
29. Materials in this section are taken from Clement E. Vose: "NAACP Strategy in the Covenant Cases," *Western Reserve Law Review* 6: 101–45 (Winter 1955) and from Professor Vose's paper, "The Impact of Pressure Groups on Constitutional Interpretation," delivered at the annual convention, American Political Science Association, Chicago, Illinois, Sept. 8, 1954.
30. *Corrigan* v. *Buckley*, 271 U.S. 322 (1926).
31. See, for example, *Hansbery* v. *Lee*, 311 U.S. 32 (1940).

32. Undoubtedly some of these articles and books would have been published without the action of the NAACP. The state-control-of-the-offshore-oil group also used this tactic. After the Supreme Court decided against them in the California case, but before the Texas and Louisiana decisions, many critical articles were published in law reviews, especially in those states which had offshore oil, and bar association journals. These were cited to show that the California decision was contrary to the weight of "informed opinion."
33. *Shelley* v. *Kraemer,* 334 U.S. 1 (1948).
34. *Slaughterhouse Cases,* 16 Wallace 36 (1873).
35. *Munn* v. *Illinois,* 94 U.S. 113 (1877).
36. *Davidson* v. *New Orleans,* 96 U.S. 97 (1878).
37. *Chicago M. & St. P. R. Co.* v. *Minnesota,* 134 U.S. 418 (1890).
38. See Edward S. Corwin: *Liberty Against Government,* Baton Rouge, Louisiana University Press, 1948, Chapter 4.

Chapter Six

1. In 1951 five Supreme Court justices sustained the argument of the Joint Anti-Fascist Refugee Committee that the Attorney General had improperly listed the organization as a subversive organization. (*Joint Anti-Fascist Refugee Committee* v. *McGrath,* 341 U.S. 123.) Some read the decision to mean that the Attorney General could not list organizations until they had been afforded a hearing. They argued that the entire list of organizations was thus invalid. Others argued that the decision meant only that an organization could have a hearing if it so demanded, but that the Attorney General could continue to list organizations. The late Senator McCarran had his interpretation. He wrote: "There have been some who have counseled that the entire loyalty program should forthwith be abandoned, on the ground that the Supreme Court decision has branded the loyalty program as at least un-American if not actually illegal. It is the writer's opinion that the Supreme Court has not 'invalidated' the loyalty program, and will not 'invalidate' it." "The Supreme Court and the Loyalty Program," from the *American Bar Association Journal,* quoted in *Congressional Record* 97: 685 (Aug. 9, 1951). To date Senator McCarran's interpretation appears to be the dominant one.
2. See Ernest R. Bartley: *The Tidelands Oil Controversy,* Austin, University of Texas Press, 1953; Lucius J. Barker: "Offshore Oil Politics: A Study in Public Policy Making," unpublished doctoral dissertation, University of Illinois, 1954; Phillip L. Sirotkin: "An Analysis of Congressional Attitudes Toward Supreme Court Decisions," unpublished doctoral dissertation, University of Chicago, 1951.
3. *McCollum* v. *Board of Education,* 333 U.S. 203 (1948).
4. *Zorach* v. *Clauson,* 343 U.S. 306 (1952).
5. See, for example, the dissenting opinions in *Lochner* v. *New York,* 198 U.S. 45 (1905); *Hammer* v. *Dagenhart,* 247 U.S. 251 (1918); *United States* v. *Darby,* 312 U.S. 100 (1941).
6. Speech before Illinois Bar Association reported in *Congressional Record* 96: A1208–10 and *New York Times,* Feb. 12, 1950.

7. *Ibid.* Among the many decisions the Senator cited as examples of judicial lawmaking were *Federal Trade Commission* v. *Cement Institute,* 333 U.S. 683 (1948); *Federal Trade Commission* v. *Hope Natural Gas Co.,* 320 U.S. 591 (1944); *Christoffel* v. *United States,* 338 U.S. 84 (1949).
8. *Youngstown* v. *Sawyer,* 343 U.S. 579 (1952).
9. *Congressional Record* 98: 6342 (June 2, 1952). The senatorial comments on this popular decision confirm Justice Miller's observation: "There is nothing within the circle of human emotions, unless it be the pleasure with which a lover praises the real or imaginary charms of his mistress, at all to be compared with the delight experienced by a lawyer glorifying a court." Charles Fairman: *Mr. Justice Miller and the Supreme Court, 1862–1890,* Cambridge, Harvard University Press, 1939, p. 142.
10. John P. Roche: "Plessy v. Ferguson: Requiescat In Pace?," *University of Pennsylvania Law Review* 103: 1: 53 (Oct. 1954).
11. *Ibid.*
12. *New York Times,* Oct. 18, 1950, p. 27.
13. 328 U.S. 303 (1946).
14. "Evasion of Supreme Court Mandates in Cases Remanded to State Courts Since 1941," *Harvard Law Review* 67: 1251–59 (1954). See also "State Court Evasion of United States Supreme Court Mandates, *Yale Law Review* 56: 574–83 (1947): "Final Disposition of State Court Decisions Reversed and Remanded by the Supreme Court, October Term, 1931 to October Term, 1940," *Harvard Law Review* 55: 357–65 (1942).
15. *Shelley* v. *Kraemer,* 334 U.S. 1 (1948).
16. *Weiss* v. *Leaon,* 359 Mo. 1054 (1949).
17. *Barrows* v. *Jackson,* 346 U.S. 249 (1953).
18. *Strauder* v. *West Virginia,* 100 U.S. 303 (1880).
19. *Norris* v. *Alabama,* 294 U.S. 587 (1935).
20. *Akins* v. *Texas,* 325 U.S. 398 (1945).
21. See for example, *People* v. *Roxborough,* 307 Mich. 575 (1943); *Hall* v. *United States,* 168 F 2d 161, and 323 U.S. 749 (1944).
22. *Hernandez* v. *Texas,* 347 U.S. 475 (1954).
23. *Burstyn* v. *Wilson,* 343 U.S. 495 (1952).
24. *Superior Films Inc.* v. *Department of Education,* 346 U.S. 587 (1954).
25. *American Civil Liberties Union* v. *City of Chicago,* 3 Ill. 2d 334 (1955); *Law Week* 23: 3244 (April 5, 1955).
26. *Sei Fuji* v. *California,* 242 P 2d 617 (1952) and cases cited therein.
27. This statement is unusually tentative and of course the existing situation may not be significantly different from the pre-1937 situation.
28. *Lonesome* v. *Maxwell,* U.S.D.C. of Md., 123 F. Supp. 193 (1954); *Holmes* v. *Atlanta,* U.S.D.C. N.D. Ga., 124 F. Supp. 290 (1954).
29. Congressman Davis of Georgia, *Congressional Record* 99: 6880–81 (June 18, 1953).
30. William O. Douglas, "Stare Decisis," *Columbia Law Review* 49: 756–57 (June 1949).
31. David Truman: *The Governmental Process,* New York, Alfred A. Knopf, Inc., 1951, p. 480.
32. *Federalist* No. 78.
33. *Composition and Jurisdiction of the Supreme Court,* Hearings before Sub-

committee of Senate Committee on the Judiciary, 83 Cong., 2d Sess., Jan. 29, 1954, p. 16.

34. *Dred Scott* v. *Sandford,* 19 Howard 393 (1857); Thirteenth Amendment.
35. *Hepburn* v. *Griswold,* 8 Wallace 603 (1870); reversed by *Legal Tender Cases,* 12 Wallace 457 (1871).
36. *Pollock* v. *Farmers' Loan and Trust Co.,* 157 U.S. 429 (1895); Sixteenth Amendment.
37. *United States* v. *E. C. Knight Co.,* 156 U.S. 1 (1895); *Swift* v. *United States,* 196 U.S. 357 (1905); *Wickard* v. *Filburn,* 317 U.S. 119 (1942).
38. *Collector* v. *Day,* 11 Wallace 113 (1871); reversed by *Graves* v. *New York ex rel. O'Keefe,* 306 U.S. 466 (1939).
39. *Hammer* v. *Dagenhart,* 247 U.S. 251 (1918); reversed by *United States* v. *Darby,* 312 U.S. 100 (1941).
40. Brooks Adams: *The Theory of Social Revolutions,* New York, The Macmillan Company, 1913, pp. 75–76.